Frank's Whales

Frank's Whales

To Tom Kohlsaat,

Enjoy!

Frank Gromling

Frank Gromling

Ocean Publishing

Flagler Beach, Florida

Frank's Whales

By Frank Gromling

Credits:
Editing: Harriette Noller
Illustrations: Jeanie Cammareri
Layout & Printing: AGP Printing, Inc.

Published by:
Ocean Publishing
Post Office Box 1080
Flagler Beach, FL 32136-1080 U.S.A.
www.ocean-publishing.com

Library of Congress # 20022113368

Copyright © 2003 by Frank Gromling

ISBN, print ed.   0-9717641-1-5

Printed in the United States of America

Contents

Preface

This book has two purposes: to tell about the fun and educational opportunities of being part of a marine conservation program, and to educate more people about the plight of the North Atlantic right whale. I am hopeful that the enjoyment that I experienced as a volunteer in the 2001 and 2002 Right Whale Watch Programs will be obvious and make this book fun to read. Although I had never been a volunteer in an animal conservancy program, I had supported such efforts and contributed financially to similar worthwhile programs protecting manatees, dolphins, and other marine creatures. This, however, was my first contribution of time and energy. It will not be my last. If you want to make a difference in the protection of endangered species, enjoy meeting and getting to know other like-minded people, and like the outdoors, you will enjoy the experience of the Right Whale Watch Program.

The second purpose of this book, to educate more people about the plight of the North Atlantic right whale, will be achieved as readers become aware that the remaining 300-350 right whales are at risk of becoming extinct. With humans causing at least a third of their deaths through ship strikes, fishing gear entanglement, or disruption of their natural habitat, right whales are fighting an uphill battle.

Thanks for buying this book. I hope you enjoy it and will share its message with others. Most of all, I hope that you become involved in volunteer programs in your neighborhood, whether for the North Atlantic right whale or Nature's other creatures that need our help. If each of us contributes time, talent, and treasure, we can and will make a difference. As a small part of my continuing effort, a portion of profits realized from this book will be donated to worthwhile research efforts to save the North Atlantic right whale from extinction.

Frank Gromling
Beverly Beach

Acknowledgements

To Bibi, who always is there for me and supports my various adventures, no matter how far out.

To Jim Hain, Ph.D., for providing an excellent opportunity to learn, have fun, and contribute to a worthy program.

To Joy Hampp for coordinating the 2001 and 2002 Right Whale Watches.

To the staff and volunteers of Marine Resources Council of East Florida, who have operated a sighting network for right whales since 1995.

To my good friend Manny Chavez whose support and encouragement were a great help to me during the entire writing process.

To all those wonderful volunteers who made the 2001 and 2002 Right Whale Watch Programs at Marineland resounding successes, and a whole lot of fun.

All of these great people helped me as I wrote this book. However, I am solely responsible for the end result.

Chapter 1

What's a Right Whale and Why Is It Called That?

Before December 2000 I had never heard of a "right whale." I'd heard of a lot of different whales - gray, pilot, sperm, bowhead, killer, but never "right." However, starting in December 2000 I got a lesson in marine biology that changed my life forever. I became a part of a volunteer-based research effort that alerted me to the potential demise of one of the world's largest creatures, the North Atlantic right whale *(Eubalaena glacialis)*. The North Atlantic right whale got its common name from early whalers who thought it was the "right" or "correct" whale to hunt. Because it swims slowly, often near the surface and close to shore, is easy to approach, and usually does not sink when dead, it became a favorite target of whalers up to the early 20th century. If you're interested in a more detailed history of the right whale decline, several sources can be found in the Written and Internet Sources section at the back of this book.

Weighing as much as 50 tons distributed over lengths up to 55 feet, the North Atlantic right whale, also called the Northern right whale, provided abundant quantities of blubber and baleen, which were highly valued. The whale blubber provided essential oil for cooking, lighting, and lubrication, while the baleen (a substance similar to human fingernails) had more esoteric purposes, such as for fans, hairbrushes, riding crops, and ribs for umbrellas and women's corsets. From well-documented reports, it is clear that whalers in the 17th-19th centuries severely diminished the right whale population off the northeastern coast of the United States.

Whalers chased and killed these creatures until, by 1900, it is estimated that perhaps only a few dozen remained alive in the western North Atlantic. Today, the entire North Atlantic right whale population reportedly is no more than 300-350, which makes it the rarest large whale in the Atlantic Ocean. Along with their right whale cousins in the North Pacific and Southern Oceans, the right whales are among the rarest baleen whales in the world.

North Atlantic right whales have very specific migration patterns, some of which are known and some of which remain shrouded in mystery. Starting in mid-November, pregnant females, sometimes accompanied by a few non-pregnant females and an occasional juvenile, travel from the area around Nova Scotia, Canada, and Cape Cod, Massachusetts, to the only known calving grounds off southern Georgia and northeast Florida. While the pregnant females are traveling south, scientists do not know what most of the males and non-pregnant females do or where they go.

From December through early March, calves are born and nursed in the shallow coastal Georgia and Florida waters that are warmer and relatively safe. "Warmer" means temperatures in the

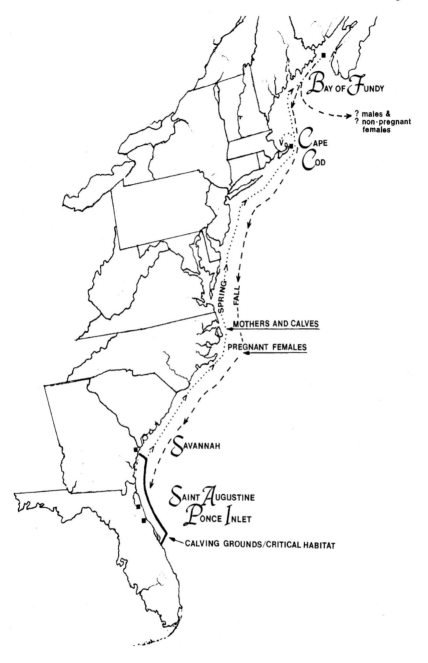

? males &
? non-pregnant
females

MOTHERS AND CALVES

PREGNANT FEMALES

CALVING GROUNDS/CRITICAL HABITAT

Migration Chart

low fifties and "relatively safe" means from their only known natural enemy, the killer whale, which does not usually inhabit the coastal shelf. This area is so important to the right whales' future that in 1994 the National Marine Fisheries Service declared it a "Critical Habitat." During this calving period, cows and calves often travel close to shore where they can be seen easily, even without binoculars, at distances less than a half-mile. March signals the return migration of the new mothers and calves to feeding and nursing areas east of Cape Cod and within Massachusetts Bay.

What prompted me to join the 2001 Right Whale Watch? Would you believe it was a whale? Here's how it happened.

In late October 2000 my wife, Bibi, and I were about to move into our new oceanfront home in Beverly Beach when I saw a whale very close to shore. My stepson, Chance, had driven from Orlando to help with final packing, and we were at the new home to check it out before the planned November 2nd move. He and I were standing on our east deck on Saturday, October 29th, just relaxing and talking.

As we chatted away, casually looking out over the ocean, I saw something large come out of the water and slap down with a powerful splash. Only 300 yards offshore, I easily recognized the black and white object as a whale's tail. To my good fortune, Chance had also seen it, so I was saved from certain derision by some of my friends who didn't believe that whales inhabited our Florida ocean waters. Some of these would-be "derisives" had lived in Flagler County most of their lives, and they'd never seen a whale offshore.

Needless to say, my curiosity was aroused. Within a couple of weeks of this sighting, a newspaper article described a public briefing about a research effort called the "Right Whale Sighting Program at Marineland." I decided to attend the December 14th meeting to see if the whale that Chance and I saw was one of these right whales. I entered the University of Florida Marine Education and Sea Grant Building with great anticipation.

We learned that this program, a collaboration between Marineland/Marine Park of Florida, the Marine Resources Council of Rockledge, Florida, and Associated Scientists at Woods Hole, Massachusetts, had its beginnings in the 1999-2000 season when the groundwork was begun by Dr. Jim Hain, a marine mammal scientist. Through slides, flip charts, graphs and personal notes, Harry Richter, of the Marine Resources Council, told us about the plight of the right whales, the most endangered marine mammal in U.S. waters. During a Q & A session, I described the whale I had seen and learned that it was a humpback, often seen while migrating through our waters. Jim Hain, Ph.D. from Associated Scientists and principal investigator for the project, and Bob Kenney, Ph.D. from the University of Rhode Island Graduate School of Oceanography, told us about scientific efforts to track right whales during their southern calving migrations.

I particularly was interested in two things that Jim Hain said, both of which involved flying. First, he mentioned that scientists were flying aerial survey trips out of north Florida in search of right whales as far north as Savannah and south to Sebastian Inlet. The aircraft they used were Cessna O-2A Skymasters, one of the aircraft I had flown in as an Air Force officer. The second item of interest was that arrangements had been made to use the Fuji blimp to search for right whales.

After all the presentations, I introduced myself to Jim, told him I had lots of experience with O-2A's and asked straight out if volunteers could ride in either the planes or, more hopefully, the blimp? I had always been intrigued by these huge airships and had wanted to fly in one for more than thirty years. He said it might be possible. "Might" was enough to clinch the deal. I signed up and went home to read the material that had been provided. Even before I finished the short drive home, I knew I was hooked!

On January 10, 2001, Jim Hain, Bob Kenney, and volunteer coordinator Joy Hampp conducted a second orientation session for about 50 people, many who were attending for the first time. We met at the Sea Grant building at Marineland again and, in a one-hour presentation, Jim and Bob delivered relatively the same material they had presented on December 14th. Jim talked about right whales in Florida, conservation and science goals, observer sighting hints, the nature of science, and the importance and role of citizen science.

Bob Kenney talked about right whale biology and their critical habitat, which he supported with lots of data and research facts. Joy Hampp explained that we also would be recording dolphin observations as part of an ancillary aspect of the whale watch program. She followed this by handing out an informative volunteer packet and explained our volunteer organization, schedule, and logistics.

We headed off for our first sight of the Marineland observation point that would become home base for us over the next seven weeks. Our observation station was the roof of the "Wonders of the Spring" exhibit, a 35,000-gallon display of underwater marvels found in a typical freshwater Florida spring. Because there were too many of us to go up on the roof at one time, Joy divided us into groups of six and then led each group to the observation station. At the top of the concrete steps that led from the ground level to the area that surrounded the top of the dolphin oceanarium, we could feel the cool ocean breeze. We followed Joy through a makeshift gate built just to allow us access to the roof while keeping out the public. Once on the roof, Joy steered us around the north side of a skylight in the center of the roof that revealed some of the water tanks in the "Wonders of the Spring" exhibit below. She told us to stay on the north side of the skylight because the roof on the south side was "not strong enough" to support our weight.

We walked to the eastern edge of the roof and looked out at the wonderful expanse of ocean and nature in front of us. We were about 30 feet above the beach, less than 100 feet away from the ocean at high tide. We had a 180° unobstructed view of the Atlantic from this rooftop perch. Joy briefly explained what was expected of us and let us look through the binoculars that we would soon be using during our watches. After talking with several volunteers, I walked back across A1A to my vehicle in front of the Marine Education Center. As I crossed the field to the parking lot, I felt confident that signing up for this volunteer program had been the right thing to do. I laughed to myself, the "right" thing to do!

As you've been reading this, you may have asked yourself, "Why are they looking for whales in the ocean from land-based locations?" Well, you're not alone in your thinking. In fact, Jim Hain brought up this question during his introduction to the future

Rooftop orientation

volunteers on December 14th. He explained that monitoring the right whales had two principal objectives: to mitigate human impact, primarily by ship strikes and gear entanglement, and to study right whale distribution, abundance, reproduction, behavior and habitat, thereby enhancing conservation and chances for recovery of the species. Numbering less than 350, and producing an average of only eleven calves a year, monitoring of the pregnant females became even more critical during the prior three years when calf births were only five or less per year.

We learned that, for more than a decade, the primary method for monitoring right whales had been through aerial surveys, where aircraft with trained observers had been flown by a number of institutions and agencies. Despite this seemingly intense approach, the aerial surveys are often only thirty-percent effective on any given day. This is due to changing weather conditions and the difficulty of sighting an animal in the ocean from 750-1,000 feet above the surface while flying at 100 mph.

We were told that a land-based observation method would provide valuable supplementary data for scientific analysis. Jim Hain said that, "In the case of a small number of animals, widely scattered, and moving in and through the area, one method - rather than go out and search for them - is to stand in one spot, and let the whales move by you." So, this was what we were going to do, let the whales come to us. Because right whales often were close to northeast Florida's shores, sometimes coming within less than a half mile, it had been decided to mount a major volunteer effort along the 42 statute miles of coastline from Matanzas Inlet, St. Johns County just north of Marineland , through Flagler County, to Ponce Inlet in Volusia County.

Volunteer networks had provided valuable information for many scientific projects in the past, including those for manatees, birds, butterflies, lobsters and more. Also, land-based observation

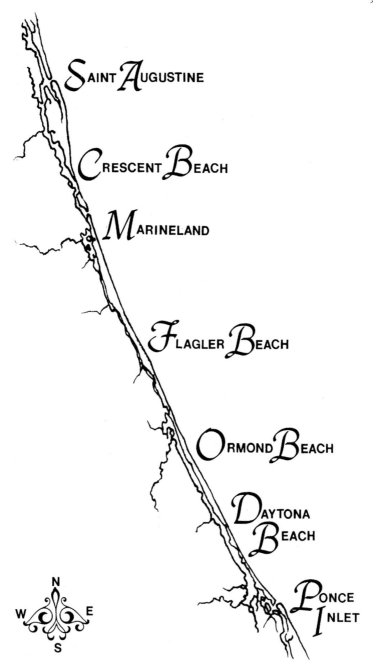

SAINT AUGUSTINE

CRESCENT BEACH

MARINELAND

FLAGLER BEACH

ORMOND BEACH

DAYTONA BEACH

PONCE INLET

N
W E
S

Our watch area

programs had been employed successfully for bowhead, gray, and humpback whales in other locales. Jim Hain told us that our future work would not be like watching the "Discovery Channel." He cautioned us that we would have long, sometimes cold, hours over several days during which there would be no sightings. He kept us captured, however, by saying that "... one or two good sightings with the associated movement and behavioral data will make the whole effort worthwhile." And what a prophetic statement that would be!

Chapter 2

How to Recognize a Right Whale

Right whales are fairly easy to recognize in their natural habitat. First, if it's December to March, and you see a large black or dark gray object floating in the ocean off northeast Florida, you've likely just seen a right whale. Well, maybe it's not quite that easy. Actually, right whales are easy to recognize in comparison with their cousins from other whale species. Right whales are one of only four species of large whales that do not have a dorsal fin. The others are the bowhead, gray, and sperm.

Right whales have black or dark gray skin and may have white patches on their chins and bellies. On the large heads of adults can be seen distinctive white or yellowish markings called "callosities." These are hardened skin areas that are covered by cyamids (whale lice) which form a unique pattern on each whale. Callosities are similar to human fingerprints; no two whales have the same patterns. Even calves develop identifiable callosity patterns shortly after birth. Once individual whales are photographed, the pictures are entered into a database at the New England Aquarium, which maintains a photographic catalogue of practically all North Atlantic right whales. From this "family album" scientists can identify the photographed whale as a known whale or register it as the first identification of a whale not previously spotted.

Whales with callosities that are basis for identification

Right whales also are recognized by their distinctive V-shaped blows. When they surface, the right whale inhales and exhales through two large blowholes on the top of its head. During the exhalation, water spouts into the air up to 15 feet in a distinctive "V" shape. This is very recognizable, even from shore.

Right whales, especially mothers and calves, spend a good deal of time at the surface, thus affording excellent opportunities for observation. Despite the fact that adults can weigh up to 50 tons and have lengths up to 55 feet, not much of this girth is visible from land. What typically is seen is only the top of the head from the snout to about 15-20 feet down a very broad back.

Very distinctive V-shaped blows

At birth calves weigh about 2,000 pounds and are 15-16 feet long. When the mother and calf are playful, periodic sightings of their short, wide pectoral flippers may be seen as they roll from side to side, often slapping the surface. Mother and calf make contact often, sometimes with the calf actually swimming onto the mother's upturned belly.

Typical sighting image of mother and calf

Another way to identify right whales is by their tail fins, called flukes, which are black on both sides, have a large center notch, and smooth trailing edges. Just prior to diving, the flukes may be visible as they're raised high into the air. Sometimes upon surfacing, the right whale will launch its head out of the water in what is called breaching, a most dramatic sight to see. All in all, these whales don't perform the dynamic acrobatics of some whale species, but they have their moments.

Right whales have earned a reputation as the "tugboat of whales." This moniker is easy to understand when one considers that a typical adult is as long as a five-story building is high, and may weigh as much as 20 American sedans. Adults have a top speed of about five miles per hour, and an average speed of 1-3 miles per hour when accompanied by calves. Because of their large oil content, the whales have positive buoyancy and find it easy to spend long

Mother with calf estimated to be only 10 days old

periods of time at the surface, especially when they are with their calves. These factors lead to a tragic aspect of the right whale story, their mortality.

If right whales get through their first three years of life, when mortality is 5-18%, they can live a long life, perhaps as long as 50-60 years. Two-thirds of right whale deaths are attributed to natural causes, such as old age, disease, and their only natural enemy – the killer whale. Unfortunately, the right whale's greatest threat comes from humans.

Because the annual calving migration occurs along the East Coast of the United States, the whales travel through and give birth in waters that are heavily used by large commercial and military ships, commercial fishing boats, and pleasure craft. The same

Short, broad flippers

Black, smooth flukes

conditions exist where right whales feed, nurse, and court off Cape Cod and Canada. Right whales, which travel slowly and often don't or can't move out of the way of fast-approaching vessels, are struck with deadly results. At least 19 right whales have died as a result of ship collisions since 1970, including two calves in 2001. While 19 deaths may not seem like a large number to some, it represents about six percent of the entire population of this colony of right whales. Suffering blunt trauma from direct ship strikes or deep lacerations from ship propellers, 30% of right whale deaths in the North Atlantic Ocean during the 15-year period prior to 1998 were caused by ship strikes.

Many agencies, including the Florida Department of Environmental Protection, New England Aquarium, Georgia Department of Natural Resources, Coast Guard, and U.S. Navy, have joined efforts to lessen ship strikes against right whales. Aerial surveys of the calving grounds, designated by the National Marine Fisheries Service as a critical habitat, record the number, size, estimated age, number of pregnant females, number of calves, and information about ship traffic. All of these data are used to determine better ways to protect the whales.

Right whale sightings are reported to the Early Warning System (EWS) central database that is maintained by the Fleet Area Control and Surveillance Facility at the U.S. Navy facility in Jacksonville. Known as FACSFACJAX, right whale sightings are logged in, and all shipping interests in Florida and Georgia waters are alerted to the whales' coordinates within a half-hour. All vessels are advised to alter course and speed to avoid striking the whales. Although ships larger than 300 tons are required to report their course, destination, and speed when they enter the Critical Habitat, compliance has been less than desired. This adds to the importance of having increased sightings to alert ships of the whales' presence.

The problem is exacerbated by the fact that much of the migration and calving activity of the right whales occurs in coastal waters that are some of the busiest in the world. There are five major commercial ports along the East Coast of the United States. Large naval facilities in Virginia and northeast Florida add an additional intense level of ship activity. Commercial fishing and pleasure boating add to the large numbers of vessels in the whales' critical habitat.

Entanglement with commercial fishing gear, primarily in northern waters, has also resulted in some right whale deaths or serious injury. Perhaps the most famous case of entanglement occurred in the summer of 2000 when a male adult right whale known as #1102, "Churchill," became entangled in fishing gear off Cape Cod. First sighted on June 8th, Churchill had a 3/4-inch thick green polypropylene line draped over his upper jaw. The line was deeply embedded and hidden by a large infection that was covered with whale lice. Despite extraordinary rescue efforts by scientists to remove the line, nothing worked. A satellite tag was implanted and Churchill was tracked until September 16th, after which no further signals were received. Scientists presume that he died far offshore in deep waters, and his body has not been recovered.

Another essential ingredient in the right whales' future is the issue of sufficient quantities of quality food sources. As right whales are baleen whales, they do not have teeth and, therefore, they do not eat fish. They feed by ingesting millions of plankton and tiny sea creatures, such as copepods and krill, plus other zooplankton. How much zooplankton and other creatures are needed to keep a 50-ton mammal alive? Would you believe at least a ton of food a day? And that's comprised of items that take about 4,000 to fill a teaspoon!

Up to 270 finely fringed baleen plates, some as large as seven feet long, are attached to each side of a whale's upper jaw. By swimming at the surface with their mouths open, baleen whales are able to filter zooplankton from the ocean as the water strains out the sides when the mouth is closed. The very long baleen of right whales enables them to trap greater amounts of zooplankton than the shorter baleen of other kinds of whales that consume both fish and larger zooplankton.

Where they feed is largely determined by the presence of large patches of zooplankton, which are massed into huge groupings by several forces, including the effects of tide or wind. Although they have several theories, scientists still do not know how right whales locate these large food patches. There is also much discussion among marine mammal scientists about the quality of food sources and their direct impact on the survivability of right whales.

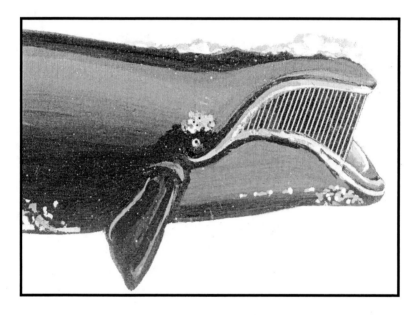

A mouth full of baleen

As with many other questions surrounding animal survival today, the issue of food quality is relevant. Scientists remain concerned about pollution of the oceans and the potential impact on food sources for the right whales. In recent years, researchers have been pleased by the apparent availability of large quantities of quality food and have attributed this, in part, to the record number of calves produced in the 2000-2001 calving season. So, while concern remains high, there appears to be no overriding problem at this time. That's refreshing news.

Not so pleasant news is the mortality report for 2001, during which seven right whales died or are presumed to have died. Of these unfortunate seven, three were adults, including a female, and four were calves. Two of the calves are known to have died as the result of ship strikes off Assateague, Virginia, and Long Island, New York.

Another part of the slow growth of the right whale population is their low reproduction rate. The mean age when female right whales first give birth is eight years. Plus, while the age of sexual maturity for males is uncertain, it is believed to be ten years. So, it is clear that there is a fairly long time between the birth of right whale calves and the time when they mature and can contribute to the population size.

Further complicating right whale resurgence is the fact that the mean interval between calf births had been 3.67 years for the period 1980-1992 and 5.8 years for the years 1990-1998. Based on new research at the New England Aquarium, this interval has increased further to a mean average of 6.2 years. Giving birth to only one calf at a time, each mature female might contribute only a few calves during her birthing capability period, which is another unknown. Scientists have spotted one mother and calf and then later identified that cow as the mother of another calf born 24 years before. So the female reproduction period is at least that long.

Right whale calf births have varied widely over the few years they have been studied. For example, from 1980 to 1992, calf births ranged from as few as five to as many as seventeen per year. The highest count prior to the record of 31 calves in 2001 was 21 calves counted in 1996. Scientists are quick to point out, however, that calf counting is not an exact science because sightings are dependent on so many variables, including weather, sufficient aerial and land-based surveillance teams, and a host of other conditions. Not the least of the problems is the unknown number of adult females capable of conceiving and delivering healthy calves.

As so many questions remain, it became more apparent to us that our land-based whale spotting activity was more important than we had imagined at the start. If we could provide just one vital piece of information that saved one mother, one calf, or one potential mother, that would be a great accomplishment.

Chapter 3

Life on the Roof

During the January 10th orientation and training program, we learned that the watch program would operate every day, weather permitting, from January 11th until February 28th. Each day would be divided into two four-hour shifts, with three to four volunteers per shift. As I had signed up for the 1:00-5:00 p.m. shift, Monday and Friday, I reported at 12:45 p.m. for my first duty on Monday, January 15th.

Because poor weather had canceled the morning watch, I helped to move four white plastic chairs and four 2-foot square sections of 1/2" plywood out to the edge of the roof of the "Wonders of the Spring" building. We laid the plywood onto the roof in a line about eight feet back from the edge, each square about two feet from the other. We then sat a chair on each square, facing east. The plywood squares were to keep our chair legs from sinking into the asphalt roof. In a few minutes Karen, the only other volunteer scheduled for the afternoon shift, arrived and introduced herself.

Ready for action

Joy explained what we were to do and how to do it. She showed us how to measure the average wind speed and highest gusts with the Kestrel 1000 pocket wind meter. With this device, we also were to determine wind direction by moving it slightly from left to right, settling on the direction from which we got the highest readings.

We also were to notice weather conditions and judge the visibility and distance to the horizon. We determined the sea condition by using the Beaufort Wind Scale. All of this information, plus any other pertinent remarks, was to be entered onto the Conditions Data Sheet every 30 minutes. Each of us was to take turns determining the facts while another volunteer recorded the collected data.

We also had a Sighting Data Sheet on which we were to record any and all whale or dolphin sightings. Although we were

Kestrel 1000 wind meter

participating in a whale watch program, we had been told that an ancillary benefit of this watch program would be the data collected from dolphin sightings. This data could help to understand their feeding, migration, and behavioral patterns in the wild.

Beside the Kestrel wind meter, the only other equipment the volunteers used were two binoculars and a stick. Of the two Nikon 7X50 binoculars, I liked the pair with a built-in compass, which was very handy for determining the direction of the wind and the bearing of any whale or dolphin spotted by the team.

The stick? Well, that was a low-tech version of a distance finder that Dr. Bob Kenney made for us. With it, we could determine a reasonably valid distance from our watch point to the sighted object, hopefully a right whale. Essentially, the device was a 5-foot long piece of wood that was 1" square. Mounted perpendicular at one end was a 5" long by 1" square piece of wood. On this short piece were five marks that represented different distances: 1/10th mile, 1/2 mile, 1 mile, and 2 miles.

Beaufort Wind Scale

Developed in 1805 by Sir Francis Beaufort of England

Force	Wind (Knots)	WMO Classification	Appearance of Wind Effects	
			On the Water	On Land
0	Less than 1	Calm	Sea surface smooth and mirror-like	Calm, smoke rises vertically
1	1-3	Light Air	Scaly ripples, no foam crests	Smoke drift indicates wind direction, still wind vanes
2	4-6	Light Breeze	Small wavelets, crests glassy, no breaking	Wind felt on face, leaves rustle, vanes begin to move
3	7-10	Gentle Breeze	Large wavelets, crests begin to break, scattered whitecaps	Leaves and small twigs constantly moving, light flags extended
4	11-16	Moderate Breeze	Small waves 1-4 ft. becoming longer, numerous whitecaps	Dust, leaves, and loose paper lifted, small tree branches move
5	17-21	Fresh Breeze	Moderate waves 4-8 ft taking longer form, many whitecaps, some spray	Small trees in leaf begin to sway
6	22-27	Strong Breeze	Larger waves 8-13 ft, whitecaps common, more spray	Larger tree branches moving, whistling in wires
7	28-33	Near Gale	Sea heaps up, waves 13-20 ft, white foam streaks off breakers	Whole trees moving, resistance felt walking against wind
8	34-40	Gale	Moderately high (13-20 ft) waves of greater length, edges of crests begin to break into spindrift, foam blown in streaks	Whole trees in motion, resistance felt walking against wind
9	41-47	Strong Gale	High waves (20 ft), sea begins to roll, dense streaks of foam, spray may reduce visibility	Slight structural damage occurs, slate blows off roofs
10	48-55	Storm	Very high waves (20-30 ft) with overhanging crests, sea white with densely blown foam, heavy rolling, lowered visibility	Seldom experienced on land, trees broken or uprooted, "considerable structural damage"
11	56-63	Violent Storm	Exceptionally high (30-45 ft) waves, foam patches cover sea, visibility more reduced	
12	64+	Hurricane	Air filled with foam, waves over 45 ft, sea completely white with driving spray, visibility greatly reduced	

Bob Kenney had determined that if a person of average height, standing on the rooftop 30 feet above the ocean, held this device at eye level, the device would be about 35 feet above the ocean. He knew that an elevation of 35 feet provides a line of sight to the horizon of about six miles. So, when we held the unit at eye level and pointed it at an object in the ocean, we determined where the horizon crossed the vertical portion and looked at the related mileage reading to know the distance to the object. Simple, right? Simple, but not very effective. In fact, the "stick" got set aside very quickly and was not used for the rest of the season.

Low-tech distance finder

Although we weren't introduced to them on our first day, we later learned that the whale watch project did have some nice electronic items that helped immensely with the project. There were three cameras: a Canon Sure Shot 105 Zoom for any close-up shots, a Canon EOS ElanIIE with a 100-400 mm lens, and a Canon EF100-400mm with zoom lens and a 1.4X telextender for greater distances.

Other equipment included two GPS (satellite-based Global Positioning System) units, a pair of ICOM marine VHF two-way radios, cell phones, and something called a "Lucas AngleStar OrthoRangerII digital protractor." Don't ask. I don't have a clue how that one works because I never saw it used, but I'm told that it determines "height of eye." There, that should answer all your questions about that.

During the remainder of my first tour of duty as a whale watch volunteer, I enjoyed the interaction with the others. We gathered and entered the data, chatted among ourselves, and scanned the broad expanse of ocean for our first right whale. As no whales had been sighted during the prior four days of the watch, we just knew that we would be the first to make a sighting. So, for four hours we braved the cold and wind to keep our eyes peeled for a right whale. However, other than the occasional bathroom break or a stop in the gift shop for much needed coffee or tea, the afternoon was uneventful. We'd been wrong about being the team to spot the first right whale. But, our interest and excitement hadn't been diminished. We all agreed that there was always the next shift!

Although the shifts at the Marineland station didn't produce a single whale sighting, it wasn't because of a lack of trying. Every day, except for bad weather, volunteers manned the rooftop station. Two to four volunteers reported for duty every shift, with each person fully expecting that he or she would spot a right whale. Then, four hours later, dejected but not defeated, the volunteers would say their good-byes amid rounds of "We'll see one next time!"

The Marineland watches gave us plenty of time to get to know one another and to learn more about right whales. We found that the time on the roof went pretty fast, except maybe on those days when it was cold and the wind was out of the north at 10-15 mph. Under those conditions, the hours dragged by, hour after cold hour. In northeast Florida, the weather in January and February is unpredictable, ranging from balmy 70s with brilliantly clear skies to cold 40s and 50s with total overcast, often followed by fast-moving fog. There was no doubt in any volunteer's mind that weather conditions were our greatest challenge.

Because we were elevated thirty feet above ground and had no protection from the wind, we needed to be dressed properly for any weather. I wore a T-shirt and sweatshirt under my jacket, plus I always had warm gloves and a hat. My feet were kept warm by thick socks and hiking boots. Being an inveterate Boy Scout, I always brought along my small Olympic sports bag that contained a nylon jacket, sweater, some Joseph's cookies (my favorite), and a bottle of water. My extra jacket came in handy on more than one occasion for a volunteer who hadn't come prepared for the conditions on the roof.

Although I had lived near the ocean my whole life, I often was amazed at how the ocean could change so drastically, and so often, during the course of just four hours. The color of the ocean might go from early morning grays to mixtures of blues and greens under the mid-day sun. A warm south wind at 9:00 a.m. could be replaced by a strong northeasterly breeze three hours later, with the resulting changes of colder air and broad bands of threatening clouds.

We watched the multitudes of sea birds go about their daily activities. Gannets, pelicans, and cormorants entertained us with their superior feeding skills. With incredible precision they crashed into the ocean, almost always emerging with fish. The occasional osprey demonstrated its claws-first approach that usually produced a fish hanging from razor-sharp talons. While the diving birds provided the excitement, the wading birds offered the humor. Watching scores of terns dance along the edge of the surf was a pleasant interlude from whale watching. Their running to and fro in search of that just right morsel was fun to watch, even for someone like me who'd spent way too many days at the beach when more serious work was waiting to be done. On almost every day we also saw shrimp boats working offshore. Usually they were anywhere from one to six miles from land. In other words, they were right in the zone where right whales were known to be. We asked whether the shrimp boat fleets were part of the whale watch efforts and were surprised to learn that the shrimp boat crews did not participate in the right whale sighting effort.

Cold weather – cold people on the roof

The only exceptions to our routine on the roof came when a whale sighting occurred elsewhere and we were told to close up shop to go to the area of the sighting. Over the seven weeks of the 2001 Right Whale Watch, I worked a total of seven half-day shifts, had two more shifts canceled by bad weather, and was called at home by Joy or Jim to help on three other days when whales were sighted. All together, I was fortunate to see a total of eight right whales.

Chapter 4

An Invention
Comes from Pain

During my first day as a volunteer I made a quick discovery: holding binoculars up to my face for long periods of time was a painful thing to do. I found the weight of the binoculars to be enough to make my arms and shoulders ache after only a few minutes. Not wanting to believe that it was just me, I sneaked sideways glances at my fellow volunteers and, to my great relief, they also were finding this simple task unpleasant.

On my way home that first day, I started thinking about what could be done to relieve the stress. I knew that whatever I came up with had to be effective while remaining absolutely simple, otherwise I couldn't make it and no one would use it. I wanted to make a device that would let me hold the binoculars but would be usable by others. That presented an immediate problem because I'm 6'2" tall and most of the other volunteers weren't. So, whatever I made had to be adjustable.

Other design requirements came to mind: lightweight enough to be carried easily, a material that wouldn't be affected by our incredibly salty ocean air, and strong enough to withstand being tossed around. Oh, and cheap enough to meet my miserly constraints! Cheap was a major factor, right up there with simple. Cheap and simple - what a concept!

Within a day or two after my second whale watch shift, I had a concept design in my head and I was ready to build my prototype. I set out to put the design into material form and in almost no time at all I produced a true masterpiece of good old American ingenuity. Well, maybe not a masterpiece, but definitely a workable product that met all the requirements I had set for it. Now, would it work?

I rushed upstairs with my invention and picked up the binoculars we keep handy for watching birds, dolphins, and passing boats. I adjusted the binocular resting peg for my height, placed the binoculars on it, and leaned my face against the eyepieces. Just like I had envisioned, I could look through the binoculars while holding the upright support at the same time. I turned to Bibi, who by now was used to my "creative talents," and asked her to give it a try. Without any problem, she adjusted the resting peg to her eye height (she's 5'2"), put the binoculars on it, and, as she was peering out at the ocean, she exclaimed, "This is great!" I was in heaven. My prototype worked, and it cost less than five bucks! Without the labor, of course.

Now, for some more fun. I made a total of three more devices and on one side of each unit, I wrote "Official Right Whale Binocular Holder" with a marking pen. Because I'd made these for Jim, Bob, and Joy, on the opposite side of each device I wrote

"The Jim Hain Model," "The Bob Kenney Model," and "The Joy Hampp Model," with "January 20, 2001," the date that I would present my invention.

Bibi with binocular holder prototype

On Saturday, January 20th, I met with Joy and her husband, Carl. I could tell they were intrigued by what they saw in my right hand. I presented the binocular holder to Joy and said, "This is your Official Right Whale Binocular Holder, the Joy Hampp Model." They cracked up. I offered that my guiding design principles had been cheap, simple, and adjustable. In what I took as a compliment, and not a cheap shot, Carl said that it looked as if I accomplished all of them.

At Jim Hain's apartment on the Whitney Laboratory campus nearby, his gaze immediately went to the two binocular holders I had brought. I presented one to Jim with the same official-sounding voice, declaring this the "Jim Hain Model." I told him that the complaints of the volunteers, coupled with my own shoulder and neck pains, created this invention. I explained my design guidelines and Jim seemed genuinely impressed. I handed him the "Bob Kenney Model" and he said that Bob had already returned to the University of Rhode Island, but that he'd tell him about it.

As it turned out, the "Official Right Whale Binocular Holders" were a hit with more than Jim and Joy. Many of the volunteers told me that they loved them. I heard comments such as, "They saved my neck!" and "I couldn't have enjoyed this as much without the poles." Because Jim started calling the holders "The Gromling Pole," many of the volunteers shortened that to "the poles." Whatever they called it didn't matter to me. I was happy that they enjoyed the use of my invention as much as I enjoyed thinking them up and making them!

Volunteer using "the pole"

A hit with the volunteers

Chapter 5

2001 Sightings!

The 2001 Right Whale Watch recorded and verified by personal observation eight sightings of fifteen right whales, including five mother and calf pairs, three adult females, and two unknown classifications. Also, we recovered the partial remains of a dead calf. I want to share with you the excitement of the four sightings that I experienced personally during the 2001 season.

Here's the schedule of our 2001 sightings:

January 18th (Thursday) – One adult far offshore about a mile south of Marineland

January 19th (Friday) – Mother and calf in south Flagler Beach

January 31st through February 2nd (Wednesday-Friday) – Mother and calf tracked from Volusia County to Flagler County and back

February 6th (Tuesday) – Mother and calf pair remained stationary for nine hours in Ponce Inlet, Volusia County

February 8th (Thursday) – Mother and calf within 150 yards of Flagler Beach Pier

February 13th (Tuesday) - Dead calf on shore in Flagler Beach

February 15th (Thursday) – Mother and calf about a half mile south of Flagler Beach Pier

February 16th (Friday) – Two adults (#1711 and #1802) off Crescent Beach, St. Johns County

February 24th (Saturday) – Two individuals off North Peninsula Recreation Area, Volusia County (unable to identify whether two adults or a mother/calf pair)

January 19th Sighting

My first opportunity to see a right whale occurred during the January 19th sighting in south Flagler Beach. I was standing just my second watch at Marineland when a citizen reported seeing two whales along South A1A in Flagler Beach. Joy and volunteers Jackie and Ellie drove to the sighting area and confirmed that the whales were a right whale mother and calf pair located less than a half mile from shore. About 10:10 a.m. my cell phone rang and Joy told me to close up the watch station at Marineland in favor of actually seeing the right whales as they moved along the shore. Volunteer Maggie and I put everything away, locked the gate, and departed in our vehicles to rendezvous with the others.

When we reached the group, which was assembled on a dune walkover, I raised the Nikon binoculars to my eyes and began to search the ocean for any signs of the whales. For a few minutes I couldn't find anything remotely resembling what I thought I should be seeing. No big creature, no V-shaped blows, no nothing. Disappointed, I lowered the binoculars and then noticed that the others also had their binoculars down and were just looking to the northeast, where the last sighting had been.

The whales had submerged below the surface and after about five minutes the group exclaimed, "There they are!" For the first time, I clearly saw the mother and her calf as they broke the surface less than a quarter mile away! For the next several minutes I was mesmerized by their actions. The mother and calf, swimming close to each other, moved very slowly, with the calf staying on the mother's right side and slightly behind her. Although mostly hidden by the mother's size, I could distinctly see the calf's head from time to time.

Despite the whales beginning to leave our vantagepoint, I could still see them interacting with one another, rolling from side to side, sending up an occasional blow, and displaying their flukes before they dived beneath the surface! I was thrilled about what I was witnessing and, for the first time, felt the excitement that we had been told would come with a sighting. Maybe this wasn't "Discovery Channel" science, but I was really pleased with what I was watching!

Because the whales continued heading north, we decided to move further up the coast to a vantagepoint ahead of them. We arrived just north of High Tides Snack Jack's restaurant from where

Whales at a distance are not easy to sight

we had a decent view of the slow-moving whales. We could see the distinctive callosities on the mother's head, just like the pictures we'd been given at orientation. We saw her short flippers as she rolled and slapped the water with them. These characteristic behaviors were important to see because they would help us spot right whales during our future watches.

The weather began to close in, making it more difficult to observe the whales. By 11:48 a.m. the wind had risen to over 15 mph, and the cloud cover was more than sixty percent. Then, without notice, both whales disappeared beneath the ocean, leaving us only a fleeting glimpse of their flukes. Despite staying on station for more than an hour, there were no more sightings of my first mother and calf. In the hopes of jumping ahead of the northbound pair, the group went north to the Flagler Beach Pier at 1:45 p.m., from where they held the watch for another hour without any success. Content with the experience of having seen my first two right whales and excited about the prospect of seeing more, I departed for home to tell Bibi about my experience. Maybe the station watch atop Marineland was cold, windy, and routine, but this part of the 2001 program was great fun! And every one of us looked forward with excitement to the next sighting, which we were sure would be on our next watch.

January 31st – February 2nd Sightings

Wednesday, January 31st, a day when I was not scheduled for a watch, became my next right whale observation opportunity. About 1:30 p.m. Joy called me at home to advise that the team was observing a mother and calf off Ormond Beach. I asked Bibi to join me, and we headed south at once. Having already been outside, I knew that it was a cold day, with a light rain, so we wore jackets and hats, and threw our rain gear into the Explorer.

When we located the team, we quickly parked and hurried to their vantagepoint at the end of Standish Street. I laughed as I approached the group because one of the volunteers was using "The Gromling Pole" to hold her binoculars. She was the only one who kept her binoculars trained on the whales while the others had to periodically raise and lower theirs because of the muscle strain on their shoulders and necks. My invention was doing its job perfectly!

We quickly spotted the whales, but they were moving north of this location. We learned that this mother and calf pair had been spotted at 10:30 a.m. by Harry Richter, of the Marine Resources Council, who was staying at the Beachcomber Inn on A1A in Daytona Beach when he reported the whales. When we arrived at 2:20 p.m., the team had been following the whales for almost an hour.

Just as we were talking, the whales disappeared. The group then began a series of moves, dubbed "leap frogging," to the north in an effort to maintain good observation points as the whales continued their northern movement. We stopped first at a pedestrian walkway in the middle of a block about a quarter-mile away. Then we moved farther north to another walkway to the beach. Because there was no parking area near the pedestrian walkway to the beach, Bibi and I parked in a commercial strip shopping center across the street. I noticed right away that the end store of this center was a Dunkin Donuts. Well, there's a time to observe whales, and there's a time to eat donuts!

Bibi and I had gotten cold while watching the whales. It was a cloudy day with drizzle and light rain, and the temperature was dropping. Although we had on jackets, hats, and gloves, we were very cold. A coffee and donut sounded just right. We took a fifteen-minute break, and, sufficiently refreshed, we headed back across A1A to resume our whale observation. After about ten minutes, we all moved again to the north tower of the Volusia County Beach Patrol.

From the tower area the whales were within clear view on a 64° bearing from our position, which already put them north of us. The seas were calm and the visibility was good for about two miles out. Farther to the east were rainstorms with occasional lightning, but the whales were within a clear viewing area from shore. We observed the whales as they appeared to be unconcerned about a man on a jet ski who zoomed back and forth a few times, never close to the whales but near enough that they would have heard the commotion. A sailboat that passed about a half-mile to the east of the whales also did not appear to bother them.

The team again jumped ahead to a position across from the Ocean Village Camper Resort, with the whales now to the southeast of us at a bearing of 120°. As we watched from this position for an hour and a half, we observed various behaviors, including flipper slapping, rolling from side to side, and fluke-raising prior to dives.

We also saw five bottlenose dolphins that appeared to be playing around the mother and calf, often zipping over and around the whales. Although Bibi and I had to leave at 5:30 p.m., the team continued its observation and photographic documentation until the daylight faded an hour later.

Northbound whale (submerged in foreground) and southbound sailboat pass within a half mile

Later that night Jim Hain called me at home to say that, based on his calculations of the whales' average speed and continued direction, they should appear off Beverly Beach Camptown about 6:30 the next morning. As this was just north of our home, I told him I would be up and alert, with binoculars in hand. On Wednesday, February 1st, I awoke at 6:00 a.m. and quickly realized that, even if the whales were about to pass within 50 feet, there was no chance to see them because it was completely dark! I waited impatiently for daylight, which didn't arrive until after seven. With my binoculars and a large cup of coffee, I stationed myself on our dune walkover. At about thirty feet above the mean high tide mark, this was a good vantagepoint to catch sight of the whales if they had continued north over night. After one and a half hours I concluded that one of four possibilities existed: I had missed them, the calculations were wrong, the whales took a different course, or they moved more slowly during the night than the day before.

Because today wasn't a scheduled watch day for me, I ate breakfast with Bibi and read some internet news reports before heading out for the Flagler Beach Post Office. About a quarter-mile south of our home I saw several people standing along A1A looking toward the northeast. I stopped and scanned the water with my binoculars and there, not more than a quarter mile offshore and just south of our home, were two whales. I observed them for a moment, determined that they were a right whale mother and calf, and called in their position to Joy on her cell phone. I called Bibi and told her to go out onto our dune walkover to see the mother and calf.

When I reached the house Bibi was on the dune walkover, binoculars on "the Gromling pole," watching the mother and calf pass our house within a quarter-mile. The whales were close enough to be seen clearly, even without the binoculars.

After the whales moved past our home, I drove to Beverly Beach Camptown, an RV park a half-mile north. The conditions for sighting were absolutely perfect. The wind was out of the northeast at about 2-3 mph, with gentle rolling seas. Although there was total cloud cover, the visibility was very good within two miles from shore, and the whales could be seen easily with the naked eye. Many campers, some with binoculars, had congregated near the beach to watch the whales. Everyone was excited about this fabulous opportunity to see nature displayed so magnificently and so near shore.

We watched the mother and calf, accompanied by 5-8 bottlenose dolphins, move gradually northward in glassy seas. The volunteers from the Marineland morning shift arrived and joined the rapidly expanding crowd. By 10:30 a.m. we had to move a half-mile north to Flagler by the Sea Oceanfront Campground. In fifteen minutes we again jumped ahead of the whales to the dune walkover at Varn Park. This vantagepoint was sufficiently ahead of the whales that we could observe them as they came north for an hour and a half. Because I had an appointment in Palm Coast, I left just as the whales came abreast of our position. The team continued to watch the whales until 5:45 p.m. when the whales were last seen more than three-quarters of a mile offshore, heading out toward deeper water.

Whales lie low in the water, with only a small portion of their considerable mass being visible

This was a great day for all of us. Starting with my call of the sighting, the day progressed through several excellent opportunities to view and document mother and calf activities within plain sight of land. We believe that these two whales were actually the same pair that we tracked the day before as they moved from Daytona Beach to northern Flagler County, a distance of some eighteen miles. We had seen the whales doing a variety of actions: rolling side to side, breaching and sending up distinctive V-shaped blows, interacting with dolphins, diving with flukes extended upwards, and even performing a belly-up maneuver. This was our version of the "Discovery Channel!"

The next day, February 2nd, a mother and calf pair heading south was sighted by several people in the Ormond Beach area, including members of the Volusia County Beach Patrol. The whales were headed south, but the poor weather conditions made sightings difficult. Unfortunately, our team was not able to see the pair. Because the whales were heading south, and the timing was right, we believed this was the same pair that we had tracked during the prior two days.

February 16th Sighting

My next chance to observe right whales came two weeks later on Friday, February 16th. Although I was to report for the afternoon watch at Marineland, Joy called about 12:30 p.m. to tell me that I should come to Crescent Beach where the team was following two adult right whales that were heading south. I decided not to join the team at their location in favor of a position slightly south. I remembered a high dune walkover, near the Spyglass Condominium, that would provide an excellent observation point. If the whales continued south, I would have them in sight for at least an hour from this position, and the team no doubt would join me on this high perch.

Atop the walkover I could see the group about a quarter mile up the beach. Training my binoculars on the whales, I was excited to see how close to shore they were, well within a quarter mile of the beach. I watched the whales for a few minutes and looked back at the team to see what they were doing. I could see that volunteer Tom Hury had put on his wet suit and taken a kayak off the carrier on top of his Jeep. I realized that Tom was going to paddle out to take pictures of the whales, probably in the hope of identifying them through the right whale registry at the New England Aquarium.

Unlike other days, the weather was really cooperating with this adventure. It was mostly sunny, with the southeast wind only 4-5 mph. As Tom shoved off from the beach, he had no difficulty slicing through the small waves near shore. He quickly caught up to the whales and cautiously began taking pictures. After about thirty minutes Tom paddled back to shore where everyone, especially Tom, was excited about this new approach to our right whale watch efforts.

About this time, the whales had moved south until they were directly opposite my location. The team joined me on the walkover where we observed the slow-moving whales for more than two hours. Later, as I walked along the beach, stopping periodically to look through my binoculars, people on the beach asked what I was observing, and, in response, I offered them a look through my binoculars. Tourists and locals alike were impressed to see these monsters so close to shore, right here in Crescent Beach.

At 5:19 p.m. we had our last sighting of this obliging pair that had given the team more than seven hours of excellent observations and close-up photographs. As we'd seen with the whales on January 31st, this pair headed farther out and disappeared to the southeast just as daylight faded.

I need to explain that Tom was allowed to approach the whales because he was operating under a federal permit that Dr. Jim Hain had obtained for the research project. Without a federal permit, no one may come closer than 500 yards of a right whale.

Females #1711 and #1802 near Crescent Beach

Aquarium photo ID team. The rapid response was that, indeed, these were two adults, both females. Catalog #1711 was 14 years old and had been seen in Southeast waters in '87, '96 and '99; catalog #1802 was 13 years old and had been seen in these waters in '93 and '99. Upon learning that neither whale was known to have produced calves, we wondered if they were not healthy enough to produce offspring. We clearly could see places where their skin was sloughing off. Perhaps these two adult females were part of the right whales' problem, not part of their solution.

February 24th Sighting

My last whale sighting in the 2001 program came on another day when I wasn't scheduled to stand watch at Marineland. On Saturday, February 24th, a Volusia County Beach Patrol officer spotted whales twice between 2:05 and 2:45 p.m. off Ormond Beach. Jim Hain was alerted at 3:00 p.m. that either a mother and calf or two adults had been spotted off Ormond-by-the-Sea. Jim called me to ask if I could join him to verify a sighting, and, in less than ten minutes, he and I were driving south on A1A toward the reported location.

En route we learned that the whales were last seen about two miles south of the Flagler/Volusia county line, in the area of

Highbridge Road and A1A. Jim called volunteer Tom Hury to determine if he was available for a "kayak operation," but had to leave a voice message when Tom didn't answer. We arrived at the Highbridge Road pullout and began scanning the ocean. Conditions were not good: total clouds and a Beaufort Sea State 4.

Not seeing any whales, we moved about a half-mile north and parked off the road under a "No Parking" sign on the west side of the road. This stretch of road runs through the North Peninsula State Recreation Area, and parking is not allowed along the three-mile corridor. We thought we might be pardoned for this momentary intrusion in the name of science. We got our binoculars and "The Gromling Pole" and began a careful scan of the gray ocean.

Within minutes we spotted two whales less than a quarter mile offshore. Although the conditions were terrible, with strong easterly winds at 15-16 mph, we saw several strong blows, splashes, and flipper action. Within fifteen minutes, the whales had moved farther offshore, perhaps to a half-mile. Because of the weather conditions and waves, we were not able to determine whether the whales were a mother/calf pair or two adults.

About this time, Tom Hury and his friend, Rick Stevens, arrived and immediately launched two surf kayaks. Both men had a terrible time trying to get through the large breaking waves. Rick flipped his kayak, but remounted it and finally got through the 4-5 foot waves to join Tom past the surf line. From atop the dune we monitored their progress, or lack of it, as Tom and Rick paddled in the general direction of the whales. However, because the waves were so large, and the whales had such low profiles, the men could not see the whales from their kayaks. Also, we had a hard time keeping track of the whales, but we finally spotted them when they moved a little closer to shore, perhaps within a third of a mile.

We tried to direct Tom and Rick to the whales, but they couldn't understand our arm waving. We had no way to tell them which direction to take or how far to go to approach the whales. Both Tom and Rick disappeared completely from our view from time to time as they dropped into troughs between large waves. After about twenty-five minutes of battling the ocean, the men turned their kayaks toward shore and passed safely through the breaking surf to reach dry land.

As Tom and Rick were coming back in, I saw the last of the whales as they gave a large blow nearly three-quarters of a mile offshore. Once again, as the day ended, it appeared as if the whales were heading farther out to sea. Throughout our observation, we tried to identify whether the whales were two adults or a mother and calf, but we never had a clear view of them both at the same time. When we saw one whale, we often didn't see the other, so this made it difficult to compare them against each other in size, shape, and behavior. On two of the four occasions when I did see both whales, I thought that the whale that was farther away from us looked like a calf. It usually was in the same position that I had seen other calves, slightly back from the mother, tucked close by her side. Also, it didn't seem to be as big as the other whale.

However, we were there to report factual data, not what we thought or guessed. So, we couldn't state with 100% accuracy that this was a mother/calf sighting. All we could do was to add to the database about right whales by verifying that they were, indeed, right whales, and recording their behavior, the exact locations of our sighting, and the weather conditions.

We talked with Tom and Rick about their experiences in the heavy seas. While they were disappointed that they didn't get to photograph the whales, they were happy to be back on land. They said the surf was really tough to paddle through and both men were physically exhausted from the strain. Tom said that he had a hard time understanding all of our gesturing to him. Because of the large waves, fading daylight, and the almost half-mile distance between us, he didn't have a clue about what we were trying to tell him. So, after not making any progress in finding the whales, and seeing the diminishing daylight, Tom and Rick decided to head back to shore on their own. As the conditions had deteriorated greatly, this proved to be a sound decision. We all packed up our equipment and headed back north, hopeful that we would have another opportunity soon.

Chapter 6

Carcass Recovery

On Tuesday, February 13th, our whale-watching program again produced dramatic results, but this time the sighting was not a happy event like the other sightings. At 9:10 a.m. volunteer Tom Hury called to report that he and his wife, Barbara, were walking along the shore when they saw something unusual on the beach at South 21st Street in Flagler Beach. Tom said he thought it was the partial remains of a dead whale, perhaps the right whale calf that had been observed by the aerial survey team two weeks before. He was referring to the reporting of a dead right whale calf about three miles due east of the Flagler Beach Pier. Despite the intensive efforts of an aerial survey plane and a Coast Guard vessel from Ponce Inlet over the next two days, the calf never was found and was presumed to have sunk.

Although I wasn't working a shift on the 13th, Joy called to let me know about the discovery. She said that Jim Hain was responding, and I told her that I would go right away to lend a hand. Within ten minutes, I had stopped my work on the computer, put on a sweatshirt, jacket, boots, and hat. Although I hadn't been outside yet, I knew that it was a cold morning for Florida, with temperatures in the low 50s.

I arrived at the site, parked on South 21st Street, and ran across A1A and down the dune walkover to where Jim was standing in the surf guarding a mass of dull white flesh. Although the carcass was being washed ashore by an incoming tide, he wanted to make sure it didn't float away from him. He had found some sticks on the beach and had stuck them into the coquina sand in strategic places to help keep the carcass in place.

I greeted Jim and asked if he thought that this was the calf that had died off the pier. He said he thought it was, but he couldn't be certain because what we were looking at was only a small portion of what, even as a young calf, likely would have been four to five times larger. I joined in the efforts to restrain the 400-500 pound carcass. Although I first tried to do this without getting very wet, I soon realized that there was no way of rendering real help unless I went into the surf. Before I plunged in, though, I hesitated for a moment. The overpowering smell of rotting flesh was very noticeable, and I was concerned about touching the flesh for fear of coming into contact with some kind of disease.

Having thought about this on the way from home, I had reached into my vehicle's first aid kit and stuffed a pair of latex gloves into my jacket pocket before I ran down to the beach. I pulled the gloves from my pocket and started to put them on, only to have them tear apart as my fingers worked their way inside. Oh, great! The Florida sun had baked my gloves into an unusable mess. As I ripped them off and jammed them back into my pocket, I made a mental note to replace future latex gloves every couple of months. Not having them available for a dead whale carcass was

Jim and calf carcass

one thing; not having them in a human emergency was a different matter. So, disregarding the fact that I would be handling a potentially diseased carcass, I tramped into the cold water and tried to hold the whale in place. This was no easy task. The incoming tide was driven by an east wind that produced small on-shore waves. The whale carcass sloshing back and forth in the surf was pushing around the wooden stakes. Even though the remains were a small part of the original body, 15-20% of a 2,000 pound calf is still a lot of whale to handle.

Before I knew it, I was almost up to my knees. I realized then that my boots, bought for hiking in New Hampshire just two months before, would be ruined by the salt water. Well, I thought, there's a price for everything and today was my time to make a contribution. When I looked at Jim, I laughed out loud because he, too, was wet and getting wetter by the minute. An instant later he lost his footing and fell into the water onto the carcass. As the tide continued to come in, we kept moving the stakes to more effective locations around the carcass. Just as we seemed to have the whale corralled, the ocean had a different plan, pushing the carcass this way and that. We just kept moving the stakes.

Joy and Carl Hampp arrived soon, along with the volunteers who had been on watch at Marineland. Jim told us that the Florida Marine Research Institute in Jacksonville had been advised and a research associate was enroute. By this time we had plenty of opportunity to look more closely at the carcass. We observed that all of the whale's black skin, except for a small patch of about thirty-six square inches, was sloughed off or had been eaten off, possibly by birds. Also clearly visible were the classic semi-circle bite marks where sharks had been eating. The white remains in front of us had only a few identifiable parts, including two chest flippers, the upper jaw just past the two blowholes, a section of the belly, a large piece believed to be the tongue, and several unidentifiable pieces of blubber.

Shark bites and only skin section clearly visible

Flipper and Jaw

We found several sections of rope on the beach and tied them together to fashion a large loop. By working the loop around the parts of the carcass, the rope helped us keep the whale in place. Then, with more effort required than I could imagine, we started to drag the carcass parts higher up the beach, out of the surf. As we did this, some of the other parts were carried away by the surf, washing ashore 15-20 yards down the beach.

Jim and I repeated the looping and dragging process on one fairly large piece and succeeded in bringing it back to where we had dragged the other parts out of the water. When we got there, we were huffing and puffing heavily from the exertion of hauling several hundred pounds of carcass. I told Jim that there was no way I could do this again and again for the remaining pieces. When we put the loop around another piece of carcass, I suggested that we drag it back by taking it first back into the ocean, and then along the beach, using the natural buoyancy of the whale carcass to make our work easier. In fact, the accompanying picture from an article in

60

The <u>Daytona Beach News-Journal</u> shows Jim and me, along with Cyndi Thomas from the Florida Marine Research Institute, hauling a whale section through the surf.

By this time several people had arrived to see what all the commotion was about. Vehicles were parked along the roadside above the beach, and spectators lined the top of the sand dune. In short order, a Flagler Beach police officer arrived and had the drivers move their vehicles to side streets off A1A. More people gathered in small groups, up wind of the carcass, and some edged closer to get a better view of the pieces.

Right whale remains discovered

FLAGLER BEACH — The carcass of a baby right whale was found on the beach Tuesday.

Whale experts believe it was the same dead whale that was spotted floating in the waters of Flagler Beach a little more than two weeks ago.

While the carcass was covered with shark bite marks, the remains were so decomposed that a necropsy, or a determination of death, seemed unlikely, said Joy Hampp, a volunteer coordinator with the Whale Watching program in Marineland.

The remains, however, were sliced into pieces and taken to the Florida Marine Research Institute in Jacksonville for analysis.

Cyndi Thomas, a research assistant from the Florida Marine Research Institute, said a DNA sample could determine the mother of the calf. The 300 right whales of North America have been identified and catalogued by scientists.

News-Journal/Jacque Estes

Whale watcher volunteers Jim Hain, left, and Frank Gronling, and Cyndi Thomas, a marine research assistant from Jacksonville, drag remains of a baby right whale out of the surf Tuesday.

Every winter, the endangered whales migrate to the coastal waters of Georgia and Florida to have babies, according to the institute.

Sixteen calves, including the dead whale found Tuesday, have been born so far this year. It is the largest number of births since 19 were born in 1997, scientists said. Only six or seven new calves have been born each season in recent years, scientists said.

<u>The Daytona Beach News-Journal</u>, February 14th

After we re-located all of the whale parts to a safe place on the beach, Cyndi Thomas, from the Florida Marine Research

Institute, carefully looked over the remains and began her important work. She decided that, although the extensive decayed condition likely would prevent knowing the cause of death, a necropsy (animal autopsy) would be performed in Jacksonville that might provide a DNA match with the mother.

Cyndi put on thick rubber gloves and took out what looked like a 14-16" kitchen knife and a sharpening rod. After putting a keen edge on her knife, she sliced key portions of the carcass into manageable sections. Jim and I helped Cyndi by holding the carcass in place while she moved around it to make her cuts. This was not an easy job for her and several times she had to stop to re-sharpen her knife, dulled by the thick blubber.

News-Tribune/Jacque Estes

Flagler County whale watchers examine a dead whale calf that washed up Wednesday on Flagler Beach. Although the loss of the calf upset the crew, they said the sightings of many whales along Flagler County beaches is a positive sign.

Whale watchers find dead calf on beach

The Daytona Beach News-Journal

Finally, Cyndi, Jim and several on-lookers started the difficult task of carrying the pieces up the beach to the back of Cyndi's pickup truck. A few non-descript pieces of blubber that remained were buried in the soft beach sand. By this time, I was exhausted, so I didn't help with the carrying. I caught my breath and, after talking with Jim, Joy and Carl, I departed for home to sterilize my hands and take a long, hot shower. On the short drive north I thought to myself, "This was a great adventure! I wonder what will be next?"

(At a May 9, 2002 meeting of right whale experts and one interested volunteer in Fernandina Beach, Florida, Cyndi Thomas told me that a necropsy was not conducted because the condition of the calf's carcass was so decomposed that analysis was impossible.)

Chapter 7

Party Hardy

When we received the "Marineland Right Whale Station Update" for February 23rd we learned that an "End of Season" get-together was planned for 6:00-9:00 p.m. on March 1st at the Sea Grant Building. We were to bring our favorite foods and drink and wear our favorite Caribbean, Hawaiian, or "Parrothead" shirts.

Bibi decided to make a Spanish dish called paella, a combination of chicken, scallops, shrimp, and sausage prepared in a spicy tomato sauce. Not owning a shirt that fit the classifications Jim and Joy had set, I added my best New Orleans straw hat to a sport shirt and slacks combination, while Bibi wore a pretty floral print dress she had bought in Hawaii.

At 6:00 p.m. the Marine Education and Sea Grant building already was alive with people, music, and chatter. The large conference room where we had received our orientations had been set up with three rows of tables and chairs, plus there were four tables at the side of the room on which the food, drinks, ice, plates, and utensils were arranged. We walked around the tables and placed Bibi's paella pan next to other delicious-looking entrees.

We moved around the room, and I introduced Bibi to everyone I had gotten to know during the program. Bibi and I staked out a table and soon were joined by others with whom I had stood watch. Bibi had brought a bottle of white wine, so we opened it, shared it at the table, and relaxed into friendly talk.

The time passed quickly and, after dessert, Jim Hain stood and quieted the gathering. He told us how much he appreciated the good work that we had done and that he was proud to be associated with us. He got some good-natured boos and Bronx cheers, along with a lot of applause. He continued by telling us that he had some slides to show, and that he and Joy had some door prizes to hand out. This got a big cheer from the group.

The lights were lowered and Jim narrated a slide show that thrilled everyone. Beautiful color slides showed the right whales that had visited our waters during the past two months. We saw some of the mother/calf pairs we had tracked, the two adults off Crescent Beach, and the calf carcass found in Flagler Beach. Also included were slides of the volunteers, which brought laughter and cheers from the group. There was even a slide of the "Official Right Whale Binocular Holder," aka "The Gromling Pole."

After the slide show, Jim announced that in honor of such an important occasion as the end of the 2001 Right Whale Watch, it was only fitting that a "personality" should hand out the door prizes. With that, he said, "Ladies and gentlemen, Miss Flagler Beach!" At that moment, Joy, who had been absent for awhile, entered the room dressed in a long wig and a beach cover with the image of a shapely girl in a bikini on it! She hammed it up with Jim, who introduced her as "Erline, Miss Flagler Beach." Joy/ "Erline" pranced around and generally camped it up with theatrical enthusiasm, all to the delight of the volunteers.

Door prizes were awarded to those volunteers lucky enough to hold the ticket halves that matched the numbers drawn from Carl's straw hat. With great fanfare, "Erline" handed out the prizes, some of which were really cool. In addition to 8X10 color photos of whales we'd tracked, I especially liked the 2001 Right Whale Watch T-shirts that were given to each volunteer.

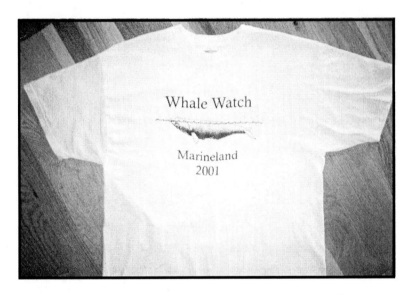

Our prized T-shirt

After the final prize was distributed, I had a surprise for Jim, who was caught off guard when I presented him with the "Second Generation" version of the binocular holder. Jim had complained, partially in jest, partially not, that he'd really like the binocular holder a lot more if he didn't have to hold the binoculars. In other words, he just wanted to hold the pole and binoculars with one hand, which would allow him to warm his other hand in his pocket!

Jim receives his 2nd generation "pole"

After some figuring and re-figuring, tempered by my original restrictions of cheap and simple, I came up with the second-generation unit that allowed the binoculars to rest on a horizontal support bar, thereby requiring only one hand to hold it upright. From "intensive" testing, I had designed the resting piece to accommodate most binocular sizes, while remaining fully adjustable for volunteers of all heights. The group laughed and applauded as Jim accepted his gift. The party ended shortly after this, and we all left with warm memories and thoughts about next year's right whale watch.

Chapter 8

A New Season – A New Approach

In a November 2001 e-mail, Jim Hain intimated that he had plans that called for me to have, as Jim put it, "an increased role" in the 2002 Right Whale Watch. I didn't know what he meant by this, but I was game for anything.

Since the end of the 2001 program, I had given a lot of thought about how we could improve our efforts. I knew that we needed to recruit people who lived in high rise condominiums along the ocean to be spotters for us. From their homes, they could watch the ocean for right whales and report their sightings to the toll-free number provided by the Marine Resources Council. I selected high rise buildings in Volusia, Flagler, and St. Johns counties that were about a mile apart and at least two floors tall.

Another idea I had was to identify all of the vehicle and pedestrian access points to the ocean in Volusia County. At first I made notes as I traveled A1A on my way to Ormond Beach or Daytona Beach on business or pleasure. I knew there had to be a better way than trying to jot down a street name every time I noticed a new access point. That was when I called the information number for Volusia County and learned that the Department of Leisure Services (I'm not making this up) had a map and list of exactly what I wanted, all readily available from its web site. I downloaded the information, printed out a copy, and made the web site a "favorite" on my computer for future reference.

On December 5th, Joy Hampp sent an e-mail message to a few veterans of the 2001 Right Whale Watch who had contributed a large amount of time and effort. She asked Paul Van Lengen, Tom Hury, and me to have an expanded role in the 2002 program. From Joy's message, it was clear that she again would be our Project Coordinator. She explained that the 2002 Right Whale Watch would be very different. Unlike 2001 when we had just one whale watch station, in 2002 we would put several teams out along the coastline to look for whales at several pre-selected locations. Joy said the teams, which would go out early in the day, would be coordinated through volunteers called team leaders, each of whom would have a number of volunteers assigned within specific areas. Joy told us that we had been selected for this team leader function because of our past commitment and experiences in the program. She said that Jim Hain would arrive on December 9th for several days of planning and coordinating and suggested that, if we were interested, we could meet during that time.

Also on December 5th, Joy sent an e-mail to everyone who had worked in the 2001 program to announce that the 2002 whale watch was about to get underway. She advised that the first orientation and training session for volunteers would be held on Tuesday, December 11th, at the Marine Education Center (the dome building). Joy also mentioned the new look for the 2002 program – survey teams rather than a stationary rooftop approach.

First Orientation and Training Session

The first orientation and training meeting on December 11th highlighted how this year's program would be very different. Not just in terms of how we would look for whales, but also how I would be involved. I arrived at 9:30 a.m., thirty minutes early, and walked into the conference room to find Jim Hain setting up the front of the room. He and Harry Richter, from the Marine Resources Council and a speaker from last year's orientation, were arranging visual displays. I said hello to Jim and Harry, and met the others who were nearby: Maia McGuire and Janet Zimmerman. Maia, a Ph.D., was the new Sea Grant Extension Agent, and Janet was the Education Coordinator for, hold onto your hat, the Guana Tolamato Matanzas National Estuarine Research Reserve. For some reason, most folks just refer to it as GTMNERR.

Anyway, as I looked around I noticed that the speakers' names were listed on a chalkboard at the front of the room. There was Harry Richter, Jim Hain, Joy Hampp, and Frank Gromling. Frank Gromling? What was this? When Jim and I had talked a few days before, he hadn't said anything about me speaking today, or any day. Why was my name on the board? I hadn't prepared anything to say. I didn't have anything to say! I looked over at Jim, who just smiled as he came up to me and handed me a 3 X 8 card on which he had outlined what he wanted me to talk about. I looked at the card again, perhaps to confirm that I really had read it correctly. As I looked at it, I wondered how could I put a talk together in just a few minutes."

FRANK

PLACARD & PHONE CARD
DISTRIBUTION

BUILDING & NEIGHBORHOOD
COORDINATORS
➡ FRANK

FRANK KEEP LIST
NAMES, BUILDINGS,
& LOCATIONS

WHICH BUILDINGS & AREAS
COVERED

WHERE "HOLES" ARE

DISTRIBUTED SIGHTING
EFFORT

FINALIZE 1/08

Shanghaied! I know when I've been had, and Jim had just done a good job. I now noticed that the room was about half-filled with people, some of whom I knew from last year. My name was in print in front of about thirty people. How could I back out? Exactly what Jim had figured. He knew that I wouldn't bail out. As I turned to find a place to sit and collect my thoughts, I saw Joy coming into the room. Holding out Jim's card and pointing to my name on the board, I asked, "Did you know about this?" Her response surprised me. She admitted that Jim had talked with her the night before about my being a speaker at the meeting.

After Jim Hain welcomed everyone, Harry Richter described the plight of the right whales and how this land-based program fit into the observer activities of the Marine Resources Council. He said that this might be a good calving year because there may be 50-60 females capable of conception and there had been good food sources during the summer and fall. Harry said that whales already spotted by the aerial survey teams appeared to be well-fed and healthy. He cautioned, however, that if the weather stayed warmer than usual, the females may decide to have their calves farther north, around Georgia and North Carolina, where the water will not be as warm as Florida's. Our typical winter water temperature is between 50-55° Fahrenheit, but at this early point in the season, the temperatures were still in the mid-sixties.

Jim then took over and started by saying that one of the criticisms of volunteer sighting networks is that the data collected is of "low value." This is because the sightings are not verified by experienced and knowledgeable people who actually go to the sighting location and confirm what has been reported. As stated earlier, confirmation of sightings is what we do best. Jim pointed out that we would again serve as the research and development lab for the sighting network. In our specific case, we would be the confirmation force for any Marine Resources Council sightings, as well as any that our team members might make. Jim presented an excellent selection of slides depicting the right whales in different circumstances, ranging from nursing calves to adults caught in nets and several with propeller cuts. He concluded his talk by telling us that our objectives were to supplement and complement the aerial surveys. Specifically, we were to increase the sighting effort, provide more and better sighting information, and foster the concept of citizen stewardship of the whales. Then Jim called on Joy to describe the way the program would work in 2002.

She explained the spotter–coordinator-surveyor concept where we needed three types of volunteers. Spotters would be anyone who lived along the coast who would report any whales they might see. Coordinators would be those who lived in an oceanfront condo or other residential community and would assist us by recruiting others within their community to be spotters or surveyors. Surveyors were those volunteers who would go out to predetermined locations to look for whales along the coast. When Joy finished, I was on.

As it turned out, I had put together an organized talk that highlighted the points that were on the card Jim had given me. I went to the front of the room and gave an animated explanation of how we were going to set up our whale watch. I described the sector concept whereby the 52 statute miles of coast from Ponce Inlet to Saint Augustine Beach would be divided into five separate sections, each approximately ten miles long. While I didn't go into detail, largely because I didn't <u>have</u> any detail, I did outline the basic steps that we would follow.

When I finished my ten-minute talk, Jim introduced Tom Hury, who was the head of our "Kayak Division." Tom described his feelings of euphoria and fear when he approached the two adult female whales in 2001. The whole group laughed heartily when he said what he was thinking when he was close to the whales: "What the heck am I doing out here?" Then he asked anyone with an ocean kayak and ocean kayak experience to talk with him later about his plans. After Tom, Jim took questions from the group and ended the session by thanking the people for the large turnout. He then asked those wanting to volunteer to sign up on the forms he circulated around the room. We spent several more minutes talking with volunteers who stayed after the meeting and, after saying goodbye to everyone, I departed for home.

The next night, December 12th, Jim called to ask me to dinner with Joy and Carl Hampp. We went to the Turtle Shack, a favorite of mine, and had an enjoyable dinner meeting during which we discussed the orientation of the day before. We all agreed that the session went well, and we were pleased with the turnout of 57 people. I told Joy, who was balancing her job with the demands of the right whale program, I would handle as much of the field requirements as I could. This meant, among other things, that I would help identify the five survey sectors between Ponce Inlet and Saint Augustine Beach. Also, I'd think about which high rise buildings could serve as spotting locations. We talked and laughed for an hour and a half before calling it a night.

Over the next few days I was very busy editing a friend's book that had a December 15th publication deadline, so I didn't work on the whale watch organization. When the book was finished, I resumed the selection of the survey and spotting locations. Once I created the initial list, I drove to each sector and verified that the chosen sites would work well for us. Several locations were changed when better sites were discovered, but overall the locations were satisfactory. I finished this preparation in time for the next planning meeting with Joy on December 19th. After ninety minutes of discussing our work on sectors, spotting and survey locations, printing, publicity, and volunteer recruiting, we agreed to meet again in a couple of weeks.

Jim dropped a bombshell on Joy and me on December 20th when he sent an e-mail to us to say that he had to delay his arrival in Florida until January 12th, four days after the planned orientation and training session. So, now Joy and I would have to conduct the January 8th orientation by ourselves. We laughed and agreed that we were more than up to the task.

On December 31st Joy and I met to review the work we each had done to date and to work out more details about how the 2002 program would unfold. Just as we were beginning our 10:00 a.m. meeting in Joy's office, her husband, Carl, called Joy on the two-way radio they used to communicate while on the Marineland grounds. From his position atop the Oceanarium, Carl reported that he saw a whale due east of the building where we were meeting. Joy and I immediately went outside to a small observation mound that put us about ten feet higher than the ground level.

Within ten minutes, we spotted a black whale less than a quarter-mile offshore. Because the skies were cloudy and the ocean was gray, we had a hard time identifying whether this was a right whale or a humpback. Then, after we saw the tail and got a glimpse of a pectoral fin, we knew we had a right whale. But, it got better. We also realized that there was a calf next to the first whale. We had just spotted a right whale mother and calf! What was so amusing to us was that during the entire 2001 right whale watch at Marineland, we did not see a single right whale from that location. And here we were at Marineland, looking at a right whale mother and calf, and the 2002 program hadn't even started! With right whales, as with everything in Nature, there was just no way to know what or when things would unfold. We observed the whales for thirty minutes and, after reaching the southern end of the new boardwalk at Marineland, we secured the watch and returned to our meeting.

Joy and I met for more than an hour. We discussed the proposed spotter and survey locations that I had researched, including distances and driving times. She explained how she envisioned the January 8th orientation and training session would be organized. We talked about what items each survey team would need, such as binoculars, cell phones, clipboards, forms, and more.

Perhaps the most difficult task was to define the roles of the team leaders. Joy and I worked well together and agreed to finish up the details later.

Second Orientation and Training Session

The second orientation and training session for volunteers was held on January 8, 2002. Joy and I had divided the presentation between us and we prepared our respective talks. She also handled the planning and arrangement of the conference room at the Marine Education Center. When I arrived a half hour early for the 10:00 a.m. presentation, practically everything had been set up. Joy was adjusting her computer and projector for her part of the presentation which would explain the plight of the right whales and the purpose of the 2002 Right Whale Watch program. About sixty chairs had been set out to face the front of the room, where several tables had been placed for materials and supplies. I arranged the items that I would be using in my part of the presentation, and then I began to greet both the veteran and new volunteers.

Joy started the meeting by welcoming everyone and describing the endangered status of the North Atlantic right whales and the history of our program. Then she explained how the 2002 approach would be different than the 2001 program where we had used only one sighting location. Joy briefly described how the rest of the program would unfold, gave some observer sighting hints, and then called on me to describe the details of the survey process.

I explained that we were seeking volunteers who would serve in one of three positions. We wanted volunteers who lived in high rise condos or two or three-story homes on the oceanfront who would call the Marine Resources Council (1-888-97-WHALE) when they saw a right whale from their homes. These "spotters" would provide important assistance by watching from high elevations.

The second type of volunteer position was the "coordinator." These people would live in a high-rise or oceanfront home, and they would help us develop their neighborhoods into an active group of spotters. The last group of volunteers would be the most active. These would be the "surveyors" who would join with others to drive along the coast in search of right whales.

I moved to the west side of the room where I had taped three maps to a large portable chalkboard. Each map was of a different county within our watch territory: St. Johns, Flagler, and Volusia. On each map I had marked the survey locations with a 1" X 3" strip of green paper that had the name of the location written on it – Ocean Trace, Varn Park, Flagler Beach Pier, Highbridge, etc. As I described the four sectors, I pointed to the green tabs and gave some indication why these places had been selected as survey locations. After some audience questions and a few remarks by me about being safe while doing the surveys, I turned the meeting back to Joy who added a few points and then concluded by thanking everyone again.

Joy then asked those who wanted to volunteer to be a spotter or coordinator to meet with me. Those wanting to be a surveyor were to meet with her and the designated team leaders. The meeting ended and the breakout groups gathered in their separate areas of the room. Thirty minutes later, the survey teams had been given their instructions, a set of forms on a clipboard with an attached pen, and an "Official Right Whale Binocular Holder" that I had prepared for them. We were ready to do our part. I wondered if the whales would do theirs.

On Wednesday, January 9th, the 2002 Right Whale Watch moved into high gear. From Ormond Beach to St. Augustine Beach, four survey teams hit the road at 8:00 a.m. to search for whales. The team leaders had prepared well. Volunteers met at pre-arranged staging points and began to monitor the ocean in front of them.

Volunteers choosing assignments

Each of the four teams had been provided with specific materials to assist them with their duties.

Each team had a Mobile Survey Data form, a Sighting form, and a clipboard with attached pen. To aid the volunteers, each team had one of my custom-built "Official Right Whale Binocular Holders" that was to be transferred each day when the clipboard was assigned to the next day's volunteers. Finally, each team was given a list of the designated survey locations within its specific territory. As part of my role in the right whale watch, I had driven the forty-eight miles of the four sectors and selected the best survey locations. Each of the sites chosen afforded an unobstructed view of the ocean. Wherever possible, the location had a dune walkover to provide an elevated platform for better viewing. All of the locations were along A1A and, to ensure our volunteers' safety, each survey location had either a vehicle pullout area or a public parking lot.

A fifth sector, from Ponce Inlet to the North County Beach Patrol tower in Ormond Beach, was staffed by Volusia County Beach Patrol officers. Because they operated from established points along this section of the coast, we did not see the need to overlap their efforts with our volunteers.

To provide assistance and encouragement to the volunteers, Joy and I agreed to oversee the teams' operations. She took Teams 1 and 2, while I took Teams 3 and 4. Almost every day of the 2002 program I drove the survey sectors from Varn Park in Flagler County to Raymonde Shores in Volusia County. I talked with the volunteers, offered sighting tips, made sure they had Sighting forms, and offered encouragement and support. After all, these great people were all volunteers who were contibuting their time, vehicles, and energies for hours at a time. We wanted to make sure that they felt both appreciated and respected.

Chapter 9

Fuji Re-visited

Do you remember the "clincher" from Chapter 1 that convinced me to join the 2001 Right Whale Watch? Yep, it was that the Fuji blimp would be used in aerial surveys and that volunteers "might" be able to fly in it. I would have signed up anyway, but the Fuji blimp was a definite inducement for me. Altough I never got to ride in the blimp, it was a major enticement and exciting possibility. Well, the 2002 Right Whale Watch would be very different in one major way. I actually got to fly in the blimp for an entire day!

Before going further, however, I have to correct two things I've said. The aircraft being written about is not a "blimp," which is a nickname passed down from the British in World War II. Rather, according to its manufacturer and flight crew, it is an "airship." Second, the name of the airship owner is not Fuji, it is Fujifilm. With that cleared up, let me tell you about the thrill of a lifetime.

I have always been in love with airplanes and flying. When I was in college, I hired a pilot and a Cessna 172 to give a girlfriend and me an aerial tour of her home town, Newport, Rhode Island. While the relationship didn't last, my love for flying did. Before the year was out, I was completing Air Force officer training, and although I couldn't be a pilot because of slightly less than perfect eyesight, I knew that I wanted to serve in the service that had the most planes. And fly I did! In four years of military time, I flew in more than twenty aircraft types, from the smallest to the biggest, props to jets. In the time since the military, I have flown in practically every U.S. and many foreign commercial aircraft over a million miles. I guess you could say that I love aircraft and flying in them.

In an e-mail message on January 11th, Jim told Joy and me that he was being offered about a week of flights on the Fujifilm airship. He said that the ship would be flying out of New Smyrna Beach and he wanted to know if we could arrange our schedules so that each of us could fly with him on different days. He actually asked the question in a serious manner, as if I might say, "No, I just can't get away." I could hardly contain myself over the possibility of finally getting an airship ride.

On January 18th Jim picked me up at 7:45 a.m., and we drove to New Smyrna Beach Industrial Air Park, where the sight of the Fujifilm airship was absolutely breathtaking. As we drove over the concrete ramp to the designated parking area, I was impressed by the large number of support vehicles and red-shirted ground personnel in front of us. All told, there were seven vehicles and 14 employees near the airship. One of the vehicles was a large truck that had a vertical mast extended from it that attached directly to the nose of the airship. I also noticed several cables connected to in-ground spikes which helped keep the craft in place.

What an impressive sight! In front of us the white and green Fujifilm airship slowly moved side to side. The craft was huge: 206 feet long, 66.6 feet high, and 50.9 feet wide. Suspended below it was a cabin, known as a gondola, which looked so inviting to me.

Worth waiting for!

After meeting with Harry Richter, from the Marine Resources Council, we carried our gear out to a staging area near the mast-truck. I wandered over to one of the crew and struck up a conversation. He told me that the ship had just arrived from its base in North Carolina, and that it would be at New Smyrna Beach for a couple of weeks before moving on to the next stop as a massive billboard across America. I questioned him about the size and weight of the airship, which I learned contained 247,500 cubic feet of helium and had a gross weight of 15,820 pounds.

More and more activity around the gondola signaled our departure. Crew members scurried around untying the fastening tethers, attaching the portable staircase, and generally making the ship ready. The pilots arrived and introduced themselves: Mike, John, and Paul. I'd learn later that Mike Fitzpatrick had been flying airships for over thirty years, while John had over fifteen years

Airship and ground support crew

Mast truck with airship attached

Airship ready to depart

experience at the helm of these behemoths of the air. Paul, assigned by his British manufacturer of airships to hone his airship flying abilities, was gaining valuable experience by flying with this veteran flight crew.

After some last minute balancing of the craft, we loaded our gear and got aboard the airship. John gave a brief safety talk: "Buckle up, stay seated, the windows are emergency exits." He turned and slid into the co-pilot's seat.

At 10:07 a.m. the twin Porsche engines that we'd heard during pre-flight tests roared to life, and we were off! At first, we moved very slowly and began to slide away from the ground. As the crew disappeared below us, the engines roared even louder, and we gained altitude at an incredible 45° angle. I was fascinated by this rapid rate of climb. Then, all at once, the engines cut back and the forward movement of the craft slowed, yet we continued to gain altitude. Paul explained later that to get the large ship moving, the powerful engines were turning at 5,200 RPM until we reached about 400 feet. Then power was reduced to a more efficient setting that allowed us to continue to rise to our flight altitude of 750 feet.

Ponce Inlet Lighthouse

As we turned to the southeast, I saw the Ponce Inlet lighthouse and the beautiful waters of the Atlantic. In only a few minutes, we were out over the ocean and heading south to a point on the charts known as False Cape, located within the Cape Canaveral reservation. Jim and I were sitting across from each other in the first two chairs. John came back and removed the large rectangular windows beside our seats. After setting up his research gear, Jim, Harry, and I began to scour the ocean for the whales that we knew were out there waiting for us to find. From our altitude of 750-800 feet, we could see everything! Although we were looking for right whales, we were recording any marine animals that we spotted. Dolphins, turtles, and sharks went onto our documentation forms, along with their relative position, distance, heading, quantity, time, and more. From time to time, I leaned out through the space where the window had been and looked straight down. I was ecstatic! This was such great fun!

At False Cape we turned around and headed north at 10:40 a.m. Operating a mile offshore, our plan was to travel as far north as St. Augustine, where we would turn back toward New Smyrna Beach. During this part of the trip, the pilots rotated positions about every hour, which gave all three of them equal time at the controls. At 11:15 a.m. John, who was alone at the controls, asked if I wanted to take the co-pilot's seat for awhile. With a big grin on my face, I slid under the control yoke and sat down. Although I was supposed to be looking for whales, I was having far too much fun to be doing that.

John and I talked about what it was like to fly this craft, and I remarked that it appeared to be similar to sailing. He smiled and acknowledged that this was true. To keep this huge airship on a reasonably straight course, the pilot had to anticipate the effects that air currents had on its massive structure. By sensing these influences, and taking gentle corrective action, the ship remained on a direct heading. Often, when sudden gusts buffeted the ship, more major corrections were needed, and other controls were adjusted. Everything was done in a subtle manner.

At one point, John let me take the yoke into my hands, while he lifted his hands off the controls. For a minute, I actually was flying an airship! Well, sort of. At least enough to brag about! Then, all too soon, I had to give the seat back to a real pilot and return to my observation point.

Traveling within a mile of the coast at only 30 knots indicated airspeed, we easily could see familiar landmarks that were part of the shore-based survey sectors. By noon we were looking at the Daytona Beach oceanfront, and we soon passed the North County Beach Patrol tower in Ormond Beach, High Tides Snack Jack's, and the Flagler Beach Pier. As we passed the pier, I got up and, leaning over John's shoulder, told him that my house was just ahead. I pointed it out, and he told me to call Bibi and tell her to come out onto our dune walkover. I pressed the autodial in my cell phone and told Bibi that we were within sight and to come outside to see us. Then John did something I never expected – he diverted us from a northerly heading and steered directly toward our home! John flew the airship on a course that took us just to the south of the house and, as we moved in between the 1:00 p.m. sun and our house, the airship cast a large shadow over the building. Then, passing on the west and north sides of the house, we turned back toward the ocean. I could see Bibi and our granddaughter, Grace, who was visiting from Savannah, standing and waving from the walkover. What an incredible experience! I thanked John many times during the rest of the flight.

Shortly after our house adventure, Jim received a cell call report of a whale sighting by the Coast Guard off the St. Augustine lighthouse. Mike Fitzpatrick returned to the pilot's seat and

Thrill of a lifetime!

Airship shadow approaching our house and walkover
Is this cool, or what?

immediately changed the airship's performance. For more than three hours, except for the diversion around my home, we had cruised at about 800 feet and an airspeed of 30 knots. Mike dropped our altitude to 400 feet which, with less head wind, allowed us to increase our forward speed by about twenty percent. We arrived at the designated coordinates of the sighting by 2:00 p.m. and began an intensive search. Jim contacted the Coast Guard for more information about its sighting and learned that three whales were spotted heading south at 12:35 p.m. This meant that the report was now more than two hours old! After ten minutes of a back and forth pattern, we headed south for twenty minutes until we made a 180° turn back to the north at Frank Butler Park. Ten minutes later we did another 180° turn back to the south. Within two minutes of this turn I spotted a right whale mother and calf heading southwest. I remember calling out, "I have whales. Eight o'clock." Jim and Harry responded by moving to the left side of the airship, where I was seated, and quickly sighted the two whales.

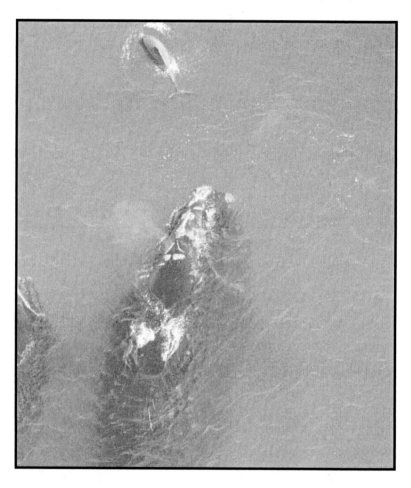

#1268 with calf (far left) with two bottlenose dolphins swimming in front - a common occurence

Mike worked to keep the airship over the pair while Jim took pictures. One time we had moved too far away from the whales while they were submerged, and we could not find them for a long time. Finally, I had an idea that maybe they were under us, so I took off my hat, leaned way out the window, and looked straight down. What a delight to see mother and calf floating gracefully below us. I yelled out that the whales were beneath us, and Mike backed the airship off to the north just far enough to give us all another great view of the whales. We followed this routine for almost an hour before Mike told us that we had to head back to the airport. Jim, sitting on the arm of his seat across from me, turned and extended his hand. Shaking hands, Jim said, "Well done, Frank, well done." So, happy that we had spotted two right whales and gotten great pictures, we departed for New Smyrna Beach.

On the return flight, I stood behind John while Paul had the controls. My eyes wandered over the flight deck and settled on a manufacturer's plaque on the panel above the co-pilot's windshield. This stainless steel sign had six advisories for the ship's pilots. As I read them, I wondered how the pilots responded when they first read these six admonishments. I laughed out loud when I read them, especially when I got to the sixth. Here they are, verbatim:

Airship approved for VFR Day and Night and IFR Day and Night Operations.

Flight in forecast or known icing conditions is prohibited.

Flight in forecast or known storm conditions is prohibited.

Flight in forecast or known lightning conditions is prohibited.

Maximum operating speed is Vmo 50 knots.

Aerobatic maneuvers are not permitted. [Emphasis added]

I swear I am not making up these advisories, especially the last one. They all are right there on a plaque screwed to the cockpit ceiling above the windshield. Before I could ask the pilots what they thought of these advisories, I was asked to sit down and buckle up for our landing. We headed straight for the southern end of the New Smyrna Beach airfield. As we banked around to line up for our descent, I could see the ground crew spread out below to direct us in and grab our tethers. Mike told us that a television news crew wanted to interview us, and I could see a cinematographer and two other men standing far outside the landing area but within filming range. By now we had turned back to the north and were descending slowly. This was like nothing I had ever experienced in an aircraft. We smoothly inched forward, lowering gradually until we were only thirty or forty feet above the ground. The engines roared and then became quieter as they were idled down. Our tether lines were grabbed, and we were held in place by the sheer strength of the crew and the maneuvering of Mike at the controls.

John told us that they were going to hover here while we got our gear and hopped off. Paul was going to get experience in taking off and landing the airship, so they wanted us to move quickly. Saying our thanks to the pilots, we stepped down the portable staircase that had been hung for us on the side of the ship. We moved briskly away from beneath the huge undercarriage of the airship, out of the way of its departure path. We stood in awe as we watched the ship lift off and head back around for another landing approach.

The three-person news crew from Channel 2, the NBC affiliate in Orlando and Daytona Beach, approached us and the reporter wanted some background about the right whale program and why the Fujifilm airship was being used for observation. Jim answered the reporter's questions on camera for about five minutes and, after some follow-up discussion, we put our gear into Jim's pickup and we headed back toward Flagler. Bibi called on my cell phone and asked, "Can you pick up some baby food for Finn on the way back?" The reality of no longer being suspended over the ocean in a marvelous airship hit hard. The reality of getting baby food for our visiting grandson brought me back to ground level. However, the excitement of this day will live forever in the mind and heart of this aviation junky. Thanks, Jim.

Chapter 10

2002 Sightings

The 54 days of the 2002 Right Whale Watch produced a total of 12 right whale sightings, including 11 of which were mother and calf pairs, and one of two female adults. The sightings were:

December 31st (Monday) - Mother and calf spotted from Marineland before actual start of 2002 Season

January 18th (Friday) - Mother (#1268) and calf spotted from Fujifilm airship off St. Augustine

January 19th (Saturday) - Mother (#1268) and calf off Beverly Beach

January 22nd (Tuesday) - Two different sightings from the Fujifilm airship near Matanzas Inlet, St. Johns County –

one pair of adults (#2330 and unknown) and one mother (#1248) and calf

January 23rd (Wednesday) - Mother (#1248) and calf sighted off south Flagler Beach by Team 4

January 27th (Sunday) - Mother (Unknown) and calf spotted in north Flagler County by Team 2

February 17th (Sunday) - Mother (#1622) and calf

February 19th (Tuesday) - Mother (#1622) and calf

February 21st (Thursday) - Mother (#1622) and calf

March 5th (Tuesday) - Mother (#1622) and calf

March 6th (Wednesday) - Mother (#1622) and calf

The following are sightings in which I was involved personally:

January 19th Sighting

After making the first whale sighting of the 2002 season from the Fujifilm airship on January 18th, I never thought I'd also make the second sighting, but that's exactly what happened on January 19th. Jim Hain had asked me to fly in the airship with him again on Saturday, January 19th. Although I had promised Bibi that I would stay with Grace and Finn while she went out for the day, Bibi knew how much the flight time in the airship meant to me. She told me to go. Specifically, she said, "Do it. It's a once in a lifetime chance." What a woman!

With Jim picking me up at 7:30 a.m., I was up and pouring a cup of coffee in the kitchen of our oceanfront home when I looked out the French doors at the ocean. At 7:08 a.m. the sun was not yet above the horizon, so the sky was a light gray, as was the ocean. What caught my eye was a 200-foot dark line in the ocean that just didn't look normal. I finished pouring my coffee and looked out again. This time the dark line, about a thousand feet out from shore, had moved slightly south and I knew then that this line was caused by something moving underneath the surface. I grabbed my binoculars and stepped out to the porch for a better look.

In an instant I saw a black form rise out of the ocean. I knew at once that I was not looking at a dolphin or shark, but at the head of a whale calf. Within less than a minute, another object surfaced just in front of and to the right of the calf. I knew that this was the mother. I now had a whale mother and calf, but did I have a right whale mother and calf? While the calf's head was sticking out of the water, the mother raised her tail high into the air for about twenty seconds before letting it fall back into the ocean. When the mother rolled gently onto her side and raised a pectoral flipper into the air, I knew without question that this was a right whale mother and calf. With a positive identification, I called Jim Hain to report my discovery at 7:13 a.m. Reaching his cell phone voicemail, I left a message of the sighting and called Joy to report what I'd seen.

Before leaving I called Jan Burweger, the Team 3 Co-Leader on duty for the weekend, so she could alert her team members that we had a sighting. This would ensure that as many volunteers as possible would get an opportunity to see right whales up close and personal. I let Bibi know about the whales and told her my plan to follow them until Jim arrived to pick me up to go to the airport. With her "Have fun!" audible behind me as I ran down the stairs to the garage, I called Jim again and left another message that he should meet me south of my home. I drove about a half mile to a point across from the Singing Surf RV Campground, from where I clearly could make out the mother and calf as they moved at the surface. I put my binoculars on the Official Right Whale Binocular Holder, which was my prototype from the 2001 season, and began to observe the whales' behavior. I started recording pertinent information – bearing, distance, heading, actions, and so on. This was difficult to do while holding the binoculars, pole, pen and writing pad.

As I alternately observed and wrote, a woman in a red Jeep pulled off A1A, parked in front of my Explorer, and approached me. "Are those right whales you're looking at?" she asked. I told her they were a right whale mother and calf pair and then, thinking she might be a volunteer that I hadn't met, I asked if she was part of the right whale watch. She said she wasn't, but that she just had read about the whales in the local newspaper and was excited about seeing them. We introduced ourselves – her name was Chris -and, handing her my note pad and pen, I asked if she'd mind being an instant volunteer. Chris laughed and immediately started writing down what I described to her: bearing, distance, heading, and so on.

Before we relocated to the next vantagepoint, Jim Hain arrived and, after observing the whales, he confirmed they were a right whale mother and calf. It was at this point that Jim threw me a curve. He told me that this was an important observation opportunity and that, because Joy couldn't supervise the tracking because of a meeting at Marineland, I should stay and oversee the events as long as possible. I looked at him in disbelief. I was thinking, "What? Miss out on another day in the Fujifilm airship? You've got to be kidding!" But, I didn't voice those thoughts and resigned myself to staying with the tracking. After all, I realized that this was what the 2002 program was all about, spotting and following right whales from shore. I was doing some heavy rationalizing.

I told Jim that I didn't have a Sighting form with me, nor did I have a GPS. He called Joy and, when he ended the call, he told me that she would bring me the forms and a GPS. With that, he said he'd call volunteer Tom Hury to see if he could replace me in the airship, and then departed for the New Smyrna Beach airport. Chris and I moved farther south to North 21st Street. From the time that Chris arrived, we had witnessed a variety of playful interactions between the mother and her offspring. The mother raised and slapped her flukes several times. At one point the calf raised its head out of the water and held it there for fourteen seconds. Then the mother raised her flukes out of the water while she was partially submerged.

We moved to a spot across from the Sea Watch Villas condominiums and continued our recording. In between taking notes and getting in an occasional glance at the whales, Chris told me that she had to go to an appointment. Before I could say anything, she added that her mother, Loretta, would be there to take over in a minute or two. I laughed out loud at how great this was. Not only had I recruited a volunteer, but I also got a volunteer's mother with the deal. Both of these wonderful people became fulltime volunteers and served through the end of the 2002 program.

Loretta arrived and took over from Chris and, together, we continued recording the activities of the whales. We moved to the side of A1A at North 16th Street and set up again. By now it was 8:20 a.m., and Joy and Carl Hampp arrived. Although I thought Joy was just going to drop off the GPS and Sighting forms for me, she was able to stay. Apparently Joy's planned meeting with a media person had been changed. With her day freed up, Joy took over the sighting and recording of data while Carl took photographs with a telephoto camera.

Soon everyone moved to North 12th Street, where several volunteers and members of the public joined us. With Joy and Carl handling things here, I decided to move on to the Flagler Beach Pier to observe the whales as they approached from the north. Because the whales had stayed on the same course for over two hours, within a thousand feet from shore, I knew that they would pass very close to the end of the pier.

When I walked out onto the pier I ran into several members of Teams 3 and 4 who were lining the rail on the north side. With binoculars raised, they were excitedly talking about what they saw and, with every tail raise, flipper slap, or V-blow, they would shout and point at the approaching whales. Volunteers, fishermen, and the public crowded the end of the pier when the mother ushered her calf past us at no more than 150 feet away. What an incredible sight everyone had of these beautiful creatures! Just fifty yards away, traveling at about one mile per hour, was a 45-foot, 50-ton animal and an 18-foot, 3-ton calf. This is what makes being a part of this program so much fun.

After the whales passed, the large group of volunteers moved together down A1A, stopping at various points to observe the whales and take pictures. By this time Flagler Beach was abuzz with the news of the whales just offshore. People in vehicles stopped along A1A and the whole scene took on the spirit of a public party. By 11:00 a.m. I had tracked the whales for almost four hours. With Joy doing the recording, and with the large number of volunteers on hand, I realized that I really wasn't needed. I decided to call it a day and return home to play with my grandchildren.

The final part to this story has an interesting wrinkle to it. As the whales passed the Flagler Beach Pier, I noticed that the mother had a bright diagonal mark on the top of her head. This identifying mark also had been on the mother whale that I had spotted the day before from the Fujifilm airship! Today's whales were the same ones that I had been the first to spot the day before, and I was the first to spot this morning. What are the chances of that happening?

Through pictures provided to the New England Aquarium, this now twice-sighted pair was identified positively as cow #1268 and her fourth calf.

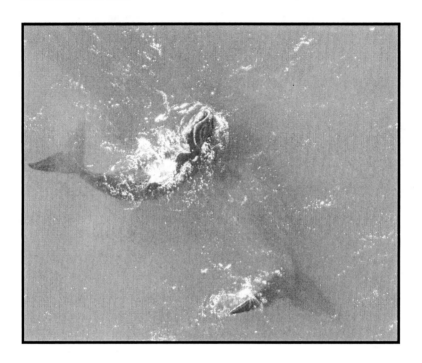

#1268 and calf, again

January 23rd Sighting

The next sighting in which I was involved came from the alert Team 4 Co-Leader, Gloria Flatly, and her husband, Bud, on January 23rd. Gloria called me at 10:08 a.m. to report what she believed to be a whale blow to the east of the High Tides Snack Jack's survey location in southern Flagler Beach. Gloria wasn't positive that it had been a blow, so I told her to watch the area closely until she actually saw a whale, or additional blows. I knew that if a whale was nearby, in a few minutes Gloria and Bud would be able to see it as it inevitably surfaced.

At 10:15 a.m. Gloria called to report that she and others on the team definitely had seen a whale and maybe two separate blows. I told her to keep tracking and I'd be right there. I decided to take our grandson, Finn, with me. Bibi dressed him, put a jacket and hat on him, and I strapped him into his car seat in the Explorer. Before leaving, I called Jim and left a message of the sighting. I said I would check it out and report back at once. I called Joy and explained my plan. Finn and I departed, and I called Gloria for an update.

She reported that two whales were in sight and moving to the south. I asked her to make sure she documented what she was observing on the Sighting form. I could almost hear her breathing stop as she realized that she had been so excited that she forgot to write anything down. I laughed and told her to start making notes and to rebuild what she had seen, and when. I asked if she had any compass headings of her sightings and she replied that she didn't have a compass. I told her to make a mark in the sand that lined up with where the whales had been and where they were now. I planned to get the bearings from her lines in the sand when I got on scene.

Finn and I arrived at Snack Jack's to find Gloria and Bud intently looking out to sea. As I asked Gloria to show me where she had recorded the bearings by making marks in the sand, Bud said that he had gotten the bearings with a handheld compass. Prior to moving farther south to jump ahead of the southbound whales, I asked Gloria to complete the data recording before she left the Snack Jack's location. I put Finn back into his car seat, and we headed to a point a half-mile away, just south of Gamble Rogers State Recreation Area.

I parked off the road at a pullout that had been the scene of several whale surveys in the past. With the windows down on the right side of the Explorer to allow me to tend to Finn in his seat, I set up my binocular pole and binoculars. Looking northeast toward where I expected the whales to be, I could not find them. Gloria and Bud arrived, along with two friends visiting from Delaware who had become caught up in the whale watch activities, and we all searched for the mother and calf. As I turned back from checking on Finn, I caught sight of the whales out of the corner of my eye. Surprised to see them directly east of us, I excitedly pointed them out to the group, which also had been looking for them farther north. Apparently the whales had sped up considerably after being spotted off Snack Jack's restaurant and were now moving quite quickly to the south.

Team 4's mother (#1248) and calf

Jim Hain arrived and I introduced him to Gloria, Bud, and their friends. I briefed him on our observations and, now holding Finn in my arms, I told him that I was going to break off from the search effort in favor of being with Finn and Grace so Bibi could do the activities she had originally planned for the day. Jim understood perfectly and began setting up his GPS, binoculars, and clipboard as I drove away. What was Finn's response to all of this activity? Before I had driven 100 yards, I turned to check on him and he was sound asleep. Maybe he'll be more interested in these endangered creatures when he's older. I learned later that this whale pair had been sighted from the Fujifilm airship the day before off Matanzas Inlet north of Marineland. It was #1248 and her fifth calf.

February 20th
False Alarm

After only very few hours of sleep, I became involved in a search effort on Wednesday, February 20th. Arriving home from the Miami International Boat Show late the night before, I hadn't had much rest when Jim Hain called at 7:45 a.m. He said that a mother and calf pair that the teams had followed the day before could be passing our home this morning. I knew that Sector 3, in which I live, did not have a survey team today because the regular volunteers were away for the month. The back-up couple was also away, and the team co-leaders were otherwise tied up with commitments. I told Jim that I would respond and handle the survey duties.

I dressed quickly, told Bibi that Jim had called about a possible whale pair coming by our home, and explained that I was going to try to find them. After checking the ocean behind our home I headed south to the North 2500 block walkover and began the search. After ten minutes, Jim arrived on his way to the Flagler Beach Airport for a day of flying in the AirCam aircraft, an experimental craft capable of very slow cruising speeds of 55-60 mph. He said that Joy would be coming to help with the search. Jim departed and I drove north to the Beverly Beach Camptown RV Resort, where I surveyed the ocean for another ten minutes. When I left the campground I called Joy to coordinate with her and we agreed that she would start her search at Varn Park and work south, while I returned to the 2500 block walkover. We did this because there was a possibility that the whales had already passed our house early in the morning and were north of where I was searching. If this was so, Joy would have a chance of picking them up at Varn Park or Flagler by the Sea Campground.

When I called the Team 3 co-leaders to advise them of the possibility of another sighting, I learned from Sue Cureton's husband that she actually was out doing the survey, at least until she had to go to an appointment at 10:00 a.m. I called Sue's cell phone, and she agreed to meet me at the walkover, where I remained a few extra minutes until she arrived. In discussing the events of the day before, Sue said that volunteer Rhonda Moon had stayed a little longer than everyone else and, even though it was getting dark, she thought the whales turned from their northward track and headed back to the south. If this was so, we all were looking in the wrong place. I immediately called Jim to advise him of this piece of information so he could begin searching farther south. Jim thanked me for the tip and said that he'd head south first and then come back north.

I decided to drive along the road and stop every 200-250 feet, rather than driving to the next survey location at 16th Street. I was confident that I would find the whales, and I didn't want to drive right by them. Hence, the stop and go technique. Joy called to say that she was moving down to the 2500 block walkover and would continue south to the Flagler Beach Pier. If she did this, I didn't need to continue south, plus I needed some breakfast and freshening up. I was tired from my late night-early morning, and I hadn't eaten anything this morning. So, I turned around and headed north toward home, stopping only to see Joy and Terran Rosenberg, Team 1 Co-Leader who had come along with Joy to search for the whales. We chatted for a few minutes and I returned home, where I ate and got some water to take with me on the rest of the survey.

Thinking that I should start a search from farther north, I decided to jump up to Varn Park and work back south. After fifteen minutes on the walkover, however, Jim called to report that he and the AirCam pilot had landed due to deteriorating weather conditions. The winds aloft had increased significantly, and by now the ocean was a Beaufort Sea State 4 and worsening. Jim said to discontinue the survey, so I packed up my gear and headed home. En route, I called Gloria Flatley, co-leader of Team 4, and advised her that Jim had called off the search for today. False alarm! All of this activity didn't turn up any whales, but we knew it had to be done in case the whales were nearby. All of us were dedicated to spotting and tracking any right whales that were within our territory, but today was a washout.

March 6th Sighting

Although the 2002 season ended officially on March 3rd, one mother and calf pair continued to roam north and south along the Flagler County coast on March 5th and 6th. My last right whale observation opportunity came on March 6th when I was called by Jim Hain, who told me that he and a volunteer were tracking a mother and calf. Cow #1622 and her calf were close to shore and heading toward me, just five miles away.

I joined Jim at the Hammock Dunes walkover, from where the whales could be seen easily just offshore. We watched in awe as the mother and calf slowly moved past our position on a southern heading. Even without binoculars we could see the mother and calf interaction. All too soon, they were south of us, forcing a change of location to Varn Park.

From this new vantagepoint, we watched the whales for about 20 minutes before they moved out of range again. As I had some work to finish, I said goodbye to Jim and returned home. I told Bibi that the whales were really close and, if they continued south, we would be able to see them as they passed east of our house. I worked on my projects for about an hour and, suddenly realizing how much time had passed, I went out onto our back deck. Within clear sight, just to the northeast of our house, I saw the mother and calf, now moving faster than they had earlier in the afternoon. I called to Bibi to join me and, together, we watched the whales make their way past our home.

I called Jim on his cell phone to invite him to stop at our home to use our back deck to get some pictures of the whales from a high platform. He and volunteer Sheila arrived within a few minutes and set up quickly to take photographs. I had set up an 8-foot stepladder to provide an even higher view of the whales. Although Jim didn't use it, Bibi found it helpful as she watched the mother and calf pass by and swim on out of range. This was a truly great way to end the 2002 Right Whale Watch – right at our own home!

Bibi watching #1622 and calf

All together, the 2002 Right Whale Watch conducted land-based surveys over a 54-day period from January 9th to March 3rd. Of the 11 sightings of whales by the volunteers, not including the "pre-season" sighting from Marineland on December 31, 2001, or the post-season sightings of #1622, ten of the sightings were close enough to provide photographic identification of the individual whales. All told, including the December 31st and March 6th sightings, I saw ten right whales during the 2002 program! I couldn't have been happier. Well, maybe just a little if I'd gotten that second day's ride in the Fujifilm airship! Overall, though, it was a super year.

#1622 heading south

Chapter 11

Fun, Fun, Fun

The 2002 Right Whale Watch was very different from the 2001 program in one other way: it had three times as many parties!

Team 2 Co-Leader Paul Van Lengen started off the festivities with an e-mail invitation to a February 1st party at his home for the volunteers in Teams 1 and 2. As I had been thinking about getting Teams 3 & 4 together for a lunch, I laughed when Paul's e-mail arrived and realized that he and I were thinking along the same lines.

Working with Team 3 & 4 Co-Leaders Sue Cureton and Gloria Flatley, we arranged a "Dutch-treat" lunch at High Tides Snack Jack's restaurant located in Team 4's territory. The owners of this restaurant were very friendly toward and supportive of our Team 4 members, even providing free coffee on cold mornings. By the end of the week we had a plan for a 12:15 p.m. lunch on January 29th. Jim Hain, Joy Hampp, and the Co-Leaders from Teams 1 & 2 were also invited.

108

On the 29th Bibi and I joined twenty volunteers on the outside patio area overlooking the ocean. Under a brilliant sunny sky, we enjoyed a variety of seafood specialties, lots of laughter, and an update by Jim Hain. It was great to listen to the excited voices and see the obvious enjoyment on the faces of the volunteers. Everyone had a great time and, as Bibi and I drove away, I remarked that this was an important part of the 2002 program that needed to be repeated soon.

Teams 3 & 4 lunchtime fun

Well, in just three days Paul Van Lengen's party got underway at his oceanside home in northern Flagler County. This Friday evening affair brought out the volunteers from Teams 1 & 2, Jim Hain, Joy Hampp, Tom Hury and me. On February 2nd Paul and his wife, Darlene, provided an excellent meal. About thirty people had a great time visiting and sharing stories about their whale watch experiences. Because Team 1 covered the new territory of St.

Augustine Beach to Matanzas Inlet, all of this team's volunteers were new to the program. Paul and Darlene's party provided a much-needed opportunity for these people to meet their counterparts in Team 2 and the others who attended. Everyone had a great time talking and sharing their individual experiences from the 2002 whale watch season to date. Leaving the party at the same time, Tom Hury and I walked to our vehicles together and agreed that this type of event was not only great fun, but an essential ingredient of a volunteer-based program. We recognized that the volunteers needed to be recognized and appreciated, and we agreed that this was a good way of doing that.

The Van Lengens' party

February passed quickly and in no time at all we were getting word about an "End of Season" party. We learned that the 2002 program would officially end on March 3rd, rather than the original date of March 10th. The e-mail announcement of the party contained a pleasant surprise for many: the party would be held in the former Dolphin restaurant and Moby Dick bar at Marineland. When Bibi and I arrived about 6:30 p.m. on March 5th, a crowd of about 70 people was already on hand. We squeezed our food contribution onto the thirty feet of buffet tables, and began to say hello to our friends. About fifteen people were standing on the former rocking boat bar, where coffee, tea, and soft drinks were arranged. Once in a while someone activated the rocking mechanism and the entire bar, including the floor where the guests were standing, would move slowly up and down, as if aboard a ship at sea. Everyone laughed and the children, who had been brought by their parents, roared with approval. After talking with Jim Hain, Carl and Joy Hampp, Tom and Barb Hury, and many others, we got our food and sat at one of the tables setup in the restaurant area in the next room.

After a dinner of good food and conversation, Jim Hain gave a slide presentation about the Right Whale Watch Program. After he described how the program began and told about the great results of the 2001 season, Jim updated everyone about the 2002 achievements. For the benefit of those who had not been involved in the program, he explained how we had four teams that covered the coast from St. Augustine Beach to Ormond Beach. Jim said that he was very pleased with the hard work and dedication of the volunteers, without whom there would be no whale watch results to report. Joy Hampp, Volunteer Coordinator, joined Jim, and they handed out gifts to some of the volunteers. Also, Jim gave several children, whose parents were volunteers, whale watch hats and other souvenirs.

I was surprised when Jim told the group that I had spotted whale #1268 and its calf on January 18th from the Fujifilm airship, and again from our home on January 19th. Then he called me up to receive a 13.5" X 18" color blow-up of the picture taken of the whales from the airship. It was at the time of Jim's handing me the large photograph that I decided on the name for this book. Up until that time, the working title had been way too long, perhaps even boring. It had been "North Atlantic Right Whales in Northeast Florida Coastal Waters." See? Long and boring! Fortunately, as Jim handed me the picture he referred to the whales as "Frank's whales." I thought to myself, that's it! "Frank's Whales" says it all. It captures my love for the right whales, my commitment to the volunteer effort, and the enjoyment I received from working with dedicated and special people – the volunteers who make the program the success it is!

"Frank's Whales"

End of Season "whale cake"

Chapter 12

What Did We Accomplish?

"We want the people who live here to feel they have a stewardship responsibility. It's the people that are going to save the whales, not the scientists."

Dr. Jim Hain

The 2001 and 2002 Right Whale Watches changed a lot of lives and, hopefully, contributed to the survival of an endangered species. Prior to this program, most of us didn't know much, if anything, about the North Atlantic right whale. In addition to expanding our knowledge about right whales, the volunteers gained greater insight about the positive impact that a few dedicated individuals can have on a worthy project.

We experienced the hands-on excitement that comes only from actually participating in a field experiment of this kind. Reading about something is just the start; the real excitement and enjoyment occurs in the getting out there and getting our feet wet! We believed that what we were doing would make a difference. This was the driving impetus for each of us.

In Jim Hain's Progress Report to the Army Corps of Engineers, dated April 3, 2001, he described the 2001 Right Whale Watch program this way:

> "In its first year, the efforts, skills, and resources of two scientists have been enhanced and multiplied by a group of 30-40 interested and dedicated volunteers. Results have been both valuable to science and conservation and rewarding to the participants."

He concluded his report by saying:

> "We found that with training, equipment, and (in particular) regular contact and reinforcement between volunteers and staff, the shore-based program provided useful results, demonstrated its merit, and provided a number of suggestions and directions for the future. The complementary goals of developing methods to supplement the aerial surveys, increasing data quality, conserving the species and its habitat, and developing broad stewardship of citizens in coastal areas have been advanced."

What more could we ask?

On top of this, we had the opportunity to meet other environmentally conscious people and some of us made new friendships that will endure. Jim and Joy know that they have a solid core of volunteers on whom they can count for future right whale watch programs. Joy told me that she was "blown away" by the response and dedication of the volunteers. She said that, for her, "The best part of the whole program was working with this group of people." and that "It was such a privilege."

We saw Jim's inventiveness and rapid ability to make adjustments to meet changing situations. His "leap frog" idea produced great results. Jim's insistence that we close up the rooftop station at Marineland in favor of having as many volunteers as possible witness actual sightings was brilliant. This gave us a better idea of the sighting image, making us better prepared for our future watches.

Speaking of inventiveness, the Official Right Whale Binocular Holder saved us all from stiff necks and tired shoulder muscles. Joy said that the binocular holder, aka "The Gromling Pole," provided some of the funniest experiences as the volunteers vied to use them, sometimes not being willing to give them up!

Because of the volunteers' work, we made an important contribution to the recovery effort of these great animals. Sure, our fourteen weeks of work weren't the same as the research projects undertaken by marine mammal scientists. Obviously our land-based program wasn't as dangerous as the aerial surveys flown out of North Florida or the boat-based research efforts that track whales at sea for days at a time. But we are proud of our accomplishments and we know that our collected data adds to the total knowledge about these endangered mammals. Each piece of the puzzle is important to understanding more about the right whales so that, hopefully, the entire picture that is pieced together is one of a species that is no longer threatened by extinction.

Perhaps Jim Hain said it best in his Progress Report for the 2002 Season:

"In summary, we have seen good progress over the course of three seasons. The VSN [Volunteer Sighting Network, i.e. our land-based volunteer program] is largely composed of local citizens participating in a local project to benefit the local environment. In many ways, the work is being accomplished that otherwise wouldn't happen (couldn't afford the time and effort now being volunteered). The young people in the program will hopefully be the informed conservationists of tomorrow. The VSN is indeed advancing the goals of adding innovation and diversity to methods employed, supplementing the aerial surveys, advancing right whale recovery and conservation, and developing essential citizenship stewardship."

We learned not only that human impact is a major threat to the right whales, but also that humans are at the forefront of critical efforts that might mitigate the whales' endangerment. While it is not yet known what favorable results may come from these human efforts, we are certain that the greater the knowledge database is about these mammals, the more likelihood there is that they will survive.

"Never doubt that a small group of thoughtful, committed citizens can change the world."

Margaret Meade

We also know that through our actions and those of volunteers in the Marine Resources Council and other observer groups, the word about the right whales' endangered situation will get out to larger and larger populations. Friends will talk with friends, newspaper and magazine articles will educate thousands, and scientific reports will present the factual justifications for greater state and federal funding of research. Will the end result of this groundswell of activity be the saving of the North Atlantic right whale? We simply don't know! Only time will provide the answer.

April 25, 2001 The Flagler Times Page 5B

Flagler Beach citizens make a difference for right whales

Residents of Flagler County helped the Right Whale Sighting Station at Marineland successfully complete its first season.

Volunteering to stand weekly four-hour shifts during January and February, they scanned the ocean with binoculars looking for the endangered right whales that come to this area each year to give birth. The volunteers maintained a dedicated watch on good weather days from atop a shore-side building at the Marineland Oceanarium along with traveling to whale sightings reported in Flagler, St.

John, and Volusia counties. Various sources alerted the Marineland Station to the presence of the whales, including government-sponsored aerial survey teams, the networks organized by Larry Long and the Marine Resources Council, individual concerned citizens and the volunteers themselves.

During the two months, Marineland Station volunteers responded to right whale sightings close enough to shore to allow them to record behavioral observations and movements of the whales. Four of those sightings took place in Flagler

Beach, making it the "hot spot" this season for viewing right whales.

Individual contributions by Flagler County citizens and the Flagler Beach City Commission greatly enhanced the value of the data collected for these whales. The City Commission supported and then expedited a temporary waiver of the walk-out fee for the Flagler Beach Fishing Pier, allowing the station's volunteers to search for and track several whales from an excellent vantage point. On February 8, a mother and her youngster drifted by the end of

the pier close enough for station volunteers to take photographs that later identified them as a previously unsighted mother/calf pair.

Staring through heavy binoculars for hours at a time made Marineland Station created a trained and committed group of local volunteers, able to provide worthwhile information to the science and management of right whales. "Creating a sense of stewardship in the people who live here is essential," said Hain. "It is ordinary citizens who will save the whales, not the scientists."

The New England Aquarium in Boston, Massachusetts reports that 26 calves were born this season, of which 24 have survived (one calf came ashore on Flagler Beach on February 13, and a second came ashore near the mouth of the Chesapeake Bay on Assateague Island, VA on March 17). This number of surviving calves is the most since monitoring of the population began in the early 1980s, and gives researchers some cause for optimism after the two poor calving seasons in 1998-1999 (three calves born) and 1999-2000 (one calf born).

In addition to developing and testing several new approaches for gathering valuable data, the Marineland Station created a trained and committed group of local volunteers, able to provide worthwhile information to the science and management of right whales.

Beach resident Frank Gromling designed and built simple, yet highly functional, adjustable and easily transported binocular supports. They became standard equipment at the Marineland Station and on whale sightings.

On February 16, operating under a federal research permit, Flagler Beach resident Tom Hury paddled out in his kayak to test the practicality of using these vessels for photo-ID work. The two 45-foot adult whales seemed unperturbed at the presence of the nine-foot craft, allowing Tom to get close enough for the photos. The two whales were identified by New England Aquarium scientists as adult females, 14 and 13 years old. Both have been sighted in this area in previous years and neither has been observed with a calf.

The Flagler Times, April 25, 2001

Unless solutions are found to the very real threats to the whales' chances for survival – ship strikes, gear entanglement, food source quality and availability, and protection of their critical habitat – there may be no North Atlantic right whales 200 years from now. On top of that, there is the very real possibility that, without sufficient breeding females right now, it may already be too late for this species. It was against these odds that the volunteers of the 2001 and 2002 Right Whale Watches made our commitments and took our places behind the binoculars, good days or bad, sightings or no sightings. We took a stand, and you know what? We're proud of our actions!

Perhaps Jim Hain said it best: "Volunteers took the program to a higher level of observer networks."

Why don't you join us? Just e-mail me (fg@gromling.com) or write to me in care of the publisher, and I'll ask the Right Whale Watch volunteer coordinator to contact you for the next program. You don't live on the East Coast of the United States or in northeast Florida? No problem, there's still lots you can do. Contact me and I'll find a volunteer opportunity for you near where you live. What are you waiting for? Get up! Go do it! Your life may be changed forever!

The Marine Resources Council

presents this certificate in recognition of the

Outstanding Volunteer Effort

of

Frank Gromling

for the

Northern Right Whale Monitoring Program

and in commemoration of reporting the seventy-sixth whale sighting on January 19 during the 2001-2002 Northern Right Whale calving season

Executive Director

March 31, 2002

Program Coordinator

Revised: 27-Feb-02

MOBILE SURVEY DATA SHEET

Date: _____   Sector: _____   Team Leader for today: _____

Page _____ of _____

Observers: _____

Location	Time Begin	Time End	Cloud (%)	WindDir	WindSpd	Beaufort Scale	Notes (feel free to continue on additional lines

Start a new sheet for each day. Times = time you begin and end observation at each location. **Cloud**=cloud cover rounded to nearest 10%. **WindDir** = approx. direction wind comes from; N, NE, E, etc. **Beaufort Scale** = Use chart provided.

Date: _____

Page _____ of _____

SIGHTING DATA SHEET

Time	Species	#	Bearing	Range	Hdng	Notes (feel free to continue on additional lines)	Obs

Start a new sheet each day.   **#** = how many animals in the group? (a range, e.g. 5-8, is OK).   **Bearing** = compass bearing (in degrees) to the sighting.   **Range** = approximate distance to the sighting.   **Hdng** = approximate direction the animal(s) is/are moving, in compass directions (N, NE, E, SE, S, SW, W, or NW).   **Notes** = activity, behavior, unique markings, presence of calf/calves.   **Obs** = your initials.

RIGHT WHALE SIGHTINGS
Phone 1-888-979-4253

Your assistance please ...

Florida and Georgia are a wintering and calving ground for the endangered right whale. There are only a total of about 300 of these animals along the U.S. east coast, with an average of 11 calves born each year. They are in the Florida/Georgia area from December to April—often within 10 miles of the coast, and sometimes within the first mile, and visible from shore.

Sightings are sparse, and very valuable – so please keep an eye out when you are on or around the ocean! Adults are dark in color, about 45 ft in length, and calves about 18 ft. The white/yellow "callosities" on the head and "nose" are your identification mark. To give you an idea of the odds—if you make one sighting per season, this would be great!!

Please record: Date, Time of Day, Location (reference to coastal fixed point, or, latitude and longitude), Number of Animals (was a calf present?) If you can get photographs to document the sighting, this would be helpful. Then, please **phone in** using the number above. Please also provide **your name and a call-back number.**

Lastly, please be cautions. Regulations forbid you from harassing a right whale or approaching within 500 yards.

Thank you.

Julie Albert, Program Coordinator,
Marine Resources Council,
Rockledge, FL 32955

Joy Hampp, Coordinator
Marineland Chapter
Marineland, FL 32080-8613

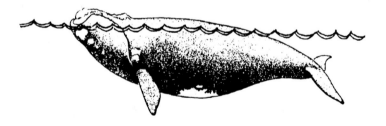

Identification Notes:
[ABOVE] Even though a right whale may be
45 ft in length, Typically only a small portion of
the head and body is exposed above water. Look
for callosities on the head, smooth black back with
no dorsal fin, and [RIGHT] V-shaped blow.

Written Sources

Published Sources

Brown, Moira W. "Gone Too Soon – The Story of the Death of a Young Right Whale." *Working for Wildlife, World Wildlife Quarterly Action Report.* Spring 1993.
The title tells the story.

Brown, Moira W. "Sex, Lies and Autoradiographs." *Whalewatcher* 25(3):13-15.
Entire issue is about right whales.

Katona, Steven K. and Scott D. Kraus. "Efforts to Conserve the North Atlantic Right Whale." In *Conservation and Management of Marine Mammals.* Twiss, J.R. and R.R. Reeves, eds. Washington, D.C.: Smithsonian Institution Press, 1999, 311-331. Succinct history of right whale demise at hands of whalers, and the international efforts to protect the whales.

Tobin, Deborah. *Tangled in the Bay: The Story of a Northern Right Whale Calf.* Halifax, Nova Scotia: Nimbus, 1999. Children's book about a right whale calf's entanglement.

Unpublished Sources

Hain, James, "Monitoring of Endangered Right Whales in Coastal Waters of Northeastern Florida by a Volunteer-Based Citizens Network." Progress Report. Army Corps of Engineers Contract No. DAC17-01-M-0080. 3 April 2001.

Hain, James, "Monitoring of Endangered Right Whales in Coastal Waters of Northeastern Florida by a Volunteer-Based Citizens Network." Progress Report. Army Corps of Engineers Contract No. DACW17-02-0047. 10 June 2002.

Internet Sources

http://floridamarine.org

Florida Marine Research Institute; contains items about Florida's efforts to protect right whales.

http://whale.wheelock.edu

Sponsored by Wheelock College, Boston, MA; sections for students, teachers and public; 1600 items on their search engine.

http://graysreef.nos.noaa.gov/rightwhalenews

Gray's Reef National Marine Sanctuary, Georgia; information about right whale history, conservation, anatomy and physiology.

www.coastalstudies.org

The Center for Coastal Studies, Provincetown, MA; disentanglement reports and satellite tracking of whale #1102, as well as other great stuff.

www.facsfacjax.navy.mil

U.S. Navy site contains current and past logs of right whale sightings in southeast critical habitat; some color pictures.

www.GEPInstitute.com

Georgia Environmental Policy Institute; obtain current and back copies of *Right Whale News* at this site. You may register to receive a free subscription by sending an e-mail request to gepi@ix.netcom.com.

www.learner.org/jnorth

Funded by Annenberg Foundation and Corporation for Public Broadcasting; resource for all kinds of species, designed for students to ask questions and follow wildlife migrations, including right whale journeys from north to south and back.

www.mrcirl.org

Marine Resources Council of East Florida; among other activities, conducts right whale sighting network of volunteers.

www.neaq.org

Lots of information from the New England Aquarium about conservation programs, right whales, etc.

www.onr.navy.mil

Office of Naval Research, U.S.Navy; excellent source in the past but, at the time of printing, no right whale information available. Visit site to inquire about future availability.

www.rightwhale.noaa.gov

"On the trail of the right whale," New England Aquarium and NOAA's National Marine Sanctuaries; has weekly mission logs and photos from tagging efforts.

www.rightwhaleweb.org

Plenty of facts, maps, pictures, videos, audio tapes and other information about the right whales provided by the North Atlantic Right Whale Consortium.

www.rightwhales.org

International Fund for Animal Welfare; info about ship strikes, entanglement, right whales, etc.

www.whoi.edu

Woods Hole Oceanographic Institute; contains information about variety of marine research programs, including right whales.

Photo Credits

Dr. Jim Hain: Cover, Pages 12, 14, 42, 45, 47, 50, 86-88, 99, 102, 106

Joy Hampp: Page 15

Tom Hury: Pages 12, 50

Paul Van Lengen: Pages 7, 24, 30, 37, 108-109, 111-112

Nielsen-Kellerman: Page 25

Frank Gromling: All others

Notes:

1. Photographs from the kayak on February 16, 2001 authorized under scientific research permit #1014 issued to Dr. Scott Kraus, New England Aquarium, by the National Marine Fisheries Service, U.S. Department of Commerce.

2. Photographs from the Fujifilm airship and AirCam aircraft authorized under scientific research permit #375-1520-1 issued to Dr. James Hain, Associated Scientists at Woods Hole, by the National Marine Fisheries Service, U.S. Department of Commerce.

Ocean Publishing
Quick Order Form

Fax orders: 386.517.2564. Send this completed form.
Telephone orders: Call 888.690.2455 toll free in USA.
Have your credit card ready.
E-mail orders: orders@ocean-publishing.com
Postal orders: Ocean Publishing, Orders Dept., P.O. Box 1080, Flagler Beach, Florida 32136-1080, USA.
Telephone 386.517.1600.

Please send me the following order of Frank's Whales:

Quantity	Price/Book	$ Total
_____	**$14.95**	$_____
	Sales Tax*	$_____
	Shipping:**	$_____
	Order Total:	$_____

*Sales Tax: Add 7% for orders shipped to Florida addresses
**Shipping: Domestic: Add $2.95 for first book and
                         $1.25 for each additional book.
               Canada: Add $3.95 for first book and
                         $2.65 for each additional book.

Payment Method: ☐ **Check**   Check number of enclosed payment: _____

☐ **Credit Card**

☐ Visa   ☐ Mastercard   ☐ American Express   ☐ Discover
Card Number: _____ Exp. Date: _____
Name on card: _____

Name: _____
Street/P.O. Box: _____
City: _____ State: _____ Zip:Code: _____
Telephone: (___) _____
E-mail address: _____

Please send free information about: ☐ Other books
     ☐ Seminars/Speaking   ☐ Consulting
     ☐ Other (Describe) _____

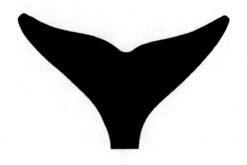

Ocean Publishing
Quick Order Form

Fax orders: 386.517.2564. <u>Send this completed form.</u>
Telephone orders: Call 888.690.2455 toll free in USA.
<u>Have your credit card ready.</u>
E-mail orders: <u>orders@ocean-publishing.com</u>
Postal orders: Ocean Publishing, Orders Dept., P.O. Box
1080, Flagler Beach, Florida 32136-1080, USA.
Telephone 386.517.1600.

Please send me the following order of <u>Frank's Whales</u>:

<u>Quantity</u>	<u>Price/Book</u>	$ <u>Total</u>
_____	**$14.95**	$_____
	Sales Tax*	$_____
	Shipping:**	$_____
	Order Total:	$_____

*Sales Tax: Add 7% for orders shipped to Florida addresses
**Shipping: Domestic: Add $2.95 for first book and
$1.25 for each additional book.
Canada: Add $3.95 for first book and
$2.65 for each additional book.

Payment Method: ☐ **Check** Check number of enclosed
payment: _____

☐ **Credit Card**

☐ Visa ☐ Mastercard ☐ American Express ☐ Discover
Card Number: _____Exp. Date:_____
Name on card:_____

Name: _____
Street/P.O. Box:_____
City:_____State:_____Zip:Code:_____
Telephone: (___)_____
E-mail address:_____

Please send free information about: ☐ Other books
☐ Seminars/Speaking ☐ Consulting
☐ Other (Describe)_____

About the Author

Frank Gromling found that owning his own businesses was a lot more rewarding and fun than being a corporate executive. Since 1980 he has owned and operated six companies, which he took from start-up to maturity. His professional and personal adventures have taken him to more than 30 countries.

Frank is founder and co-owner of The Gromling Group, Inc., a hands-on firm that conducts seminars, training, consulting, and coaching services for a variety of organizations. Also, he volunteers his time at a residential drug and alcohol rehabilitation program, where he speaks about the value of a job, and how to become successful. As a frequent speaker at teen centers, he has designed and presented "Excellence in Leadership" to help teens make positive life decisions.

Frank's Whales is his first book about nature. His other writings have included magazine articles, such as "Life is a Balance," and three texts for the U.S. Air Force: *Air Navigation, Military Aerospace,* and *Leadership.* Frank lives with his wife, Bibi, in Beverly Beach, Florida.